HUMAN RIGHTS AND WORLD ORDER

HUMAN RIGHTS AND WORLD ORDER

Edited by
Abdul Aziz Said

Transaction Books
New Brunswick, New Jersey

Library of Congress Catalog Number:
ISBN: 0-87855-718-0 (paper)
Printed in the United States of America
Library of Congress Cataloging in Publication Data

Main entry under title:

Human rights and world order.

  Includes bibliographical references.
  1. Civil rights—Addresses, essays, lectures. I. Said, Abdul Aziz.
JC571.H769 1978   323.4   78-62438
ISBN 0-87855-718-0

CONTENTS

FOREWORD—
ON HUMAN RIGHTS AND SOCIAL
OBLIGATIONS

IRVING LOUIS HOROWITZ
Rutgers University

With human rights, as with other public concerns, political events often dictate public discourse. Since the beginning of the United Nations, the question of human rights has remained in the province of UNESCO conferences; in the late 1970s it has emerged, suddenly, as a central issue. Certainly this new sense of concern cannot be explained on the basis of an intellectual breakthrough in the past thirty years. Rather, human rights have become a major instrument of American foreign policy. It should be evident that the passion for human rights is a measured response to the interests of this nation.

Yet one should not be cynical about the subject of human rights simply because the sense of concern appears so clearly related to national interests and policies. Intellectuals, and social scientists in particular, have long inhabited a world where desultory issues become dramatic events. The War on Poverty, for example, was a political invention long after the emergence of a literature on poverty; and now that particular rhetorical war has passed into oblivion, even though the realities of poverty remain. No matter how the major collective issues of the century are placed on the agenda of public discourse, the best efforts of social scientists must be put forward, however cynical one might be with respect to the national origins or even the frivolous nature of such commitments.

Politics is a game of vulnerabilities, and the human rights issue is clearly where the "socialist" world has proven most vulnerable, just as the economic rights issue is where the "capitalist" world is most open to criticism. The very interplay of forces, the competition of world historic systems and empires, provides an opportunity for quite practical mortals to gain marginal advantages over the systems they inhabit. Because of the intrinsic merit of concerns for human rights, rather than because of an effort to capitalize on a policy quirk of this specific moment in time, we offer this special volume for public discussion. The various social science disciplines have pioneered in transforming the question of human rights from a series of indecisive philosophic propositions to a precise sense of measurable statistics.

The debate on human rights can be conceptualized in part as a struggle between eighteenth century libertarian persuasions and nineteenth century egalitarian beliefs—that is, from a vision of human rights having to do with the right of individual justice before the law to a recognition of the rights of individuals to social security and equitable conditions of work and standards of living. Whether human rights are essentially a political or economic concern is not the purpose of this volume. Social science need not choose between politics and economics. It has enough on its hands to demand an accountability system involving both.

The social sciences have introduced precisely an element of accountability not only into their disciplines, but also into the policy systems and networks that social scientists find themselves in. As a result, the quantification or measurement of human rights has become the monumental contribution of social science. Big words are rightfully suspect, big concepts doubly so. It therefore becomes a central act of faith to translate the abstract into the concrete. This is largely what has been accomplished by economists, sociologists, psychologists, political scientists, and anthropologists through the use of social indicators.

The right to justice, or formal education, are concepts easy enough to absorb within the framework of almost any social system. But when rights become carefully stipulated in terms of costs, when freedom of beliefs becomes translated into freedom to impart information and ideas without harassment, when social security is translated into old age insurance, when rights to privacy are viewed as the right of every individual to communicate in secrecy, when rights to work involve the protection of workers, when social rights are translated into the rights of mothers and children to special care and protection, when rights to work involve the right to form and join trade unions and the right to strike, when rights to personal security involve measures to protect the safety of conscientious objectors, when rights to fair trials include protection against arbitrary arrest or detention—then the entire panoply of rights assumes an exact meaning that it otherwise would not have.

The habitual interest in human rights in part reflects the absence of these rights. There is a great deal of concern on matters of cruel, inhuman, or degrading treatment because there is so much cruelty, inhumanity, and degradation present in world affairs. There is concern about the rights of self-determination because there are so many violations of those rights in the name of national integration. International law calls for the punishment of genocide because the twentieth century has seen the alarming development of genocidal practices for statist ends.

There is a colossal dichotomy between practices and principles. This very split between reality and rhetoric gives the human rights issue the volatility. Yet the one enormous breakthrough that has evolved over the century is the sense of right and wrong. A common legacy of democratic and socialist systems, of libertarian and egalitarian frameworks, is the assumption that there is such a goal as human rights. When one recollects that it was only one hundred years ago that slavery and serfdom were a vital force in human affairs and that wars were fought to protect chattel slavery as state's rights, then the extent and velocity—at least conceptually—of how far we have come becomes evident.

The central characteristic of the twentieth century, what so profoundly demarcates it ideologically from previous centuries, is that a world in which obligations were taken for granted has been transformed to one in which rights are presumed to be inalienable. Our institutions were largely concerned with theories of human obligation: what individuals and collectivities owe to their societies and to their states—an automatic presumption that one has an obligation to fight in wars whatever the purpose of the war, or the notion that economic failure is a mark of individual shortcoming rather than societal breakdown. The hallmark of the twentieth century and, I daresay, the achievements of the social sciences, is to have made the question of human rights the central focus, and at the same time, to place the question of obligations on the shoulders of institutions rather than individuals.

There are risks in this transvaluation. One might well argue that the tilt has turned into a rout; that issues of the duties of individuals to the community, or the limitations of human rights to ensure national survival, have not received proper attention; that social research has so emphasized the minutae of imbalances of every sort that even homicides are now blamed on violence on television. But all transvaluations carry the potential for hyperbole and exaggeration, and there is little point in discarding the baby to purify the bathwater. The literature of the past was written in terms of dynasties, nations, and empires. As long as that was the case, the matter of human rights hardly counted. Only now, when these larger-than-life institutions—these dynasties, nations, and empires—are dissolving, can it be seen that the individual is the centerpiece of all human rights and that the expression of these rights must always remain the province of the free conscience of a free individual. In this very special sense ours is the century in which individualism has emerged beyond the wildest imaginings of previous centuries. Paradoxically, it is also the century of the most barbaric collectivisms, which put into sharp and painful relief the subject of human rights. If the momentary strategy of the political system is such that the subject of human rights now is central, the principles of social research must convert those strategies into durable gains.

PREFACE

ABDUL AZIZ SAID
The American University

H uman Rights may be difficult to define but impossible to ignore. We may quibble about the form of government, but hunger, torture, and political imprisonment are the same by any other name. Violations of human rights are not a monopoly of a single government or a group of states. They are global. The morality play of human rights reads like a dialogue of the deaf.

In the West the increasing totality of the nation-state, the declining need on the part of the state to perform the functions of security, and the integration and standardization required by technification, underscore the issue of human rights. The expanded state narrows individuality, the historical preoccupation with external security is replaced with personal insecurity, and technification obscures self-definition.

In the socialist countries the planned state economy and the emphasis upon moral and political unity has dehumanized society. The tyranny of an all-powerful party and its bureaucratic apparat has reached intolerable proportions. Socialism has become defined by production indices devoid of human considerations.

In the Third World the institutions that performed the traditional functions of social and political organizations have declined, and the new structures patterned after the Western or Marxist models have not been established firmly. While the need to satisfy and promote human rights persists, this function has not found a role in the present political system. This situation, however, cannot last; the search for dignity is an intuitive human expression.

Today's political life in the West, in the socialist countries, and in the less developed world, on the domestic level and in the global system, is not burdened by many constants. The increasing complexity of Western society, the emphasis upon greater production in socialist societies, the urge for modernization in the Third World, and the disparity in growth between rich and poor states, have ascribed higher priority to efficiency than human dignity. In the process violations of fundamental human rights have assumed global dimensions.

This volume is an effort to amplify the dialogue on human rights as a global concern. The contributors are scholars, activists, and practitioners. The essays demonstrate the deep concerns of the authors with the broad issues of human rights in the changing global environment.

The generous support of my dear friend and esteemed colleague, Irving Louis Horowitz, editor-in-chief of *Society* magazine, has been invaluable. Mary Curtis, editorial director at Praeger, and Bruce Warshavsky, editor of special studies at Praeger, have provided me with constructive criticism and sound advice. My assistants Samuel Olens, Jonathan Davis, Joel Busch, and Elizabeth Brodbine have given me a good deal of their time, thoughtfulness, and assistance. Eliot Werner, managing editor of *Society* magazine, has directed the development of this volume with efficiency and good cheer.

PURSUING HUMAN DIGNITY

ABDUL AZIZ SAID
The American University

H uman rights are concerned with the dignity of the individual—the level of self-esteem that secures personal identity and promotes human community. The Universal Declaration of Human Rights, the Convention for the Protection of Human Rights and Fundamental Freedoms, the International Covenant on Economic, Social, and Cultural Rights, and the International Covenant on Civil and Political Rights are part of the process of enlarging freedom, social justice, and the opportunity for perfectability, and the development of an environment and appropriate structures to promote these goals.

Traditional Cultures, Present Conditions

While the pursuit of human dignity is universal, its form is designed by the culture of a people. Politics is a cultural activity and reflects tradition and environment. The debate on human rights assumes that in spite of the differences which characterize the diversity of cultures, political conduct can be conceptualized by certain common norms and attitudes. In the modern global system Westerners have concentrated on discovering common denominators rooted in the Judeo-Christian traditions from which a calculus of human rights would emerge. This emphasis on Western common denominators projects a parochial view of human rights exclusive of the cultural realities and present existential conditions of Third World societies.

1

What has occurred is the reshaping of politics to accommodate various theories of political behavior gleaned from Western traditions. These theories of politics proceed from the assumption that all states share a common agenda of goals—reinforcing the perception of the universality of Western values. Western states assert their interests in an unequivocal litany of demands, including human rights; the character of these demands is determined in the crucible of the Western experience. The problem with such analogies is that they seek to reduce to formula the internal behavior of governments without examining the internal milieu, a wholly arbitrary and artificial separation of the political organism. The fact of the matter is quite different. The character and nature of human rights is determined in the crucible of a specific sociopolitical culture.

Politics is essentially an ascriptive phenomenon. It is culture specific. The goals which states maximize are a reflection of these factors. Human rights is no exception.

The development of a global conception of human rights is retarded by the lack of agreement on sources of human rights, including the very foundation of international law. The uncertainty about the content of the doctrines of human rights—including the lack of a philosophical common core—poses additional obstacles. In fact, the very conception of the organization of society differs from one culture to another. The West places more emphasis on rights, while much of the Third World values obligations. The Western tradition posits freedom in order to avoid the outcome of a despotic system, while the Third World emphasizes virtue as a goal to perpetuate tradition of society that often supports a coercive system. The West emphasizes individual interests, while much of the Third World values collective good. In the areas where natural rights transcend cultural values, as in the right to survival, the vested interests of foreign policy elites serve as a basis for disagreement in the exercise of human rights. Such political use of human rights increases the possibility of the perversion of the concept.

International Concern

The Congress of Vienna in 1815 demonstrated international concern for human rights for the first time in modern history. The congress dealt with religious freedoms as well as civil and political rights and heard petitions by individuals and groups for the international protection of those rights. Additionally, participants in the Congress agreed in principle to abolish slavery. This was followed by a number of antislavery acts and treaties: the Berlin Conference on Africa in 1885; the Brussels Conference of 1890; the Saint Germain Treaty of 1919; and the Geneva Conference of 1926. Great Britain enacted the Abolition Act of 1833 which ended slavery in the British Empire. Russia, France, Prussia, Austria, and Great Britain signed the Treaty of London in 1841 to abolish slavery. In 1845 France and Great Britain agreed to cooperate in the control of the slave trade.

The Hague peace conferences of 1899 and 1907 introduced the notion of the right of individuals to appeal to the Court of Appeal in prize (not ratified). The Central American Peace Conference of 1907 provided for the right of aliens to appeal to the courts where they resided. The problem of minorities rights, however, was heightened at the expense of other human rights such as those of women and children.

During the first two decades of the twentieth century, World War I, the efforts of peace groups, the impact of Wilson's Fourteen Points, and the Bolshevik Revolution underscored the principle of international agreement to regulate the sovereignty of states. The Peace Conference at Versailles in 1919 demonstrated its concern for the protection of minorities. Several treaties were concluded with the new states stressing minorities' rights including the right to life, liberty, freedom of religion, the right to the nationality of the state of residence, complete equality with other nationals of the same state, and the exercise of civil and political rights.

Minorities rights were placed under a system of international guarantees, with the Council of the League of Nations acting as guarantor. These rights were obligations of international interest and could not be modified without the assent of a majority of the council. Violations were to be referred to the Permanent Court of Justice. The court, however, had no binding force. Rights of individuals were not covered by the system of minorities rights. Only states could seek redress for violations of rights.

The International Labor Organization has made important contributions to the development of human rights. It has established conventions on the right to organize, abolition of forced labor, employment policy, right to collective bargaining, and discrimination in employment and occupation. The organization has been a pace setter for other specialized agencies.

The Dumbarton Oaks proposal of 1944 for the establishment of the United Nations asserted as one of the purposes of the organization to "promote respect for human rights and fundamental freedoms." Unlike the Covenant of the League of Nations, which did not refer to rights of individuals, the United Nations Charter underscores the principle of individual human rights.

The charter, however, has avoided defining rights in specific terms and has not set up adequate legal machinery to assure the effective implementation of its provisions. The role of the United Nations is further curtailed by Article 2 of the charter which upholds the concept of state sovereignty, preventing control or intervention by the United Nations in domestic matters of states. On February 16, 1946 the Security Council of the United Nations established the Commission on Human Rights and charged it with the duty of drafting an international declaration on the rights of the individual. The Universal Declaration of Human Rights was adopted by the General Assembly on December 10, 1948.

The Universal Declaration of Human Rights is an informal instrument appended to the Charter of the United Nations. Its purpose is to explain the contents of the human rights provisions of the charter and, thus, to be a preliminary formulation of the fundamental freedoms which needed recognition internationally by a series of binding covenants. It consists of thirty short articles, dealing with civil and political freedoms as well as economic, social, and cultural rights. In an effort to conciliate clashing ideologies of member states, the terms defining each right have been kept general and noncommittal.

The success or failure of international protection of human rights is contingent on state performance. Once the Universal Declaration was adopted and the standards of fundamental freedoms had been defined, there was no international obligation binding the members of the United Nations to insure the protection of these rights in their own legislations. The declaration is only a statement of general moral principles setting forth a common standard of achievement for the states of the world.

The adoption of the Universal Declaration of Human Rights necessitated a differentiation between rights and freedoms that had to be defined with legal accuracy and others that were described in general terms. This was accomplished by the drafting of two separate covenants, isolating the political and civil liberties from the economic, social, and cultural rights. The covenant dealing with the latter rights imposed on member states the duty to submit reports on their progress in the protection of human rights. The former covenant dealing with political and civil rights stimulated more extensive debates as it contemplated the creation of a nine-member Human Rights Committee to which complaints of violations could be submitted by any member state against any other signatory members.

A proposal to grant individuals the right to petition an international body for relief against a state violating their human rights was abandoned. It was feared that the covenants may become political instruments rather than effective procedures in the protection of the fundamental freedoms of individuals. Accordingly, the United Nations has persistently declined to reach any agreement which would institutionalize strong measures of international control for the protection of individual freedoms. Finally, the General Assembly unanimously approved the two covenants, one on economic, social, and cultural rights and the other on civil and political rights, on December 16, 1966.

Beyond international organizations, two regional organizations, the Council of Europe and the Organization of American States, have addressed themselves to human rights. The statute of the Council of Europe of May 1949 asserts that human rights and fundamental freedoms are the basis of the emerging European system. The signatory states affirmed "their devotion to the spiritual and moral values which are the common heritage of their peoples and the true source of individual freedom, political liberty and the rule of law." Acceptance of the provisions on human rights is a condition for membership in the Council of Europe.

The European Convention on human rights of November 4, 1950, entered into force on September 3, 1953, was the first attempt to give specific legal content to human rights in an international agreement. The European Commission of Human Rights created in 1953 and its associated bodies—the European Court of Human Rights and the Committee of Ministers—represent important progress in the area of human rights.

The commission, the court, and the Committee of Ministers review the decisions of national tribunals, but do not perform the functions of an appeal court. The deliberations of the court are secret, but the final findings are pronounced in open session. The decision of the court is not binding and the convention does not confer upon the commission the power to enforce the judgment of the court.

The institution of ombudsman is another important innovation in the area of human rights. Ombudsman is derived from "Ombud"—elected representative. It also means legal officer. The institution was created by King Charles XII of Sweden in 1713 to investigate public servants. Originally the ombudsman was appointed by the king; he later became appointed by Parliament for four years. The ombudsman must be a lawyer with the rank of a judge in the Supreme Court. Article 86 of the Swedish constitution defines the functions of ombudsman to supervise the observance of laws and institute proceedings before the courts against those who in the execution of their official duties committed unlawful acts or neglected their duties.

The Inter-American System of Human Rights is another regional model of concern for human rights. In the Declaration of Mexico of 1945 the American republics asserted the need to harmonize the rights of individuals with the interest of the community. The Declaration called on the Inter-American Judicial Council to develop a draft on the International Rights and Duties of Man. The Bogota Conference of 1948 produced the American Declaration of the Rights and Duties of Man. More than a decade later the Santiago Conference of 1959 produced the Inter-American Convention on Human Rights and provided for the establishment of the Inter-American Commission on Human Rights and the Court of Human Rights. The Inter-American Commission on Human Rights was established in 1960 and performs the following functions, as stated in Article 9 of the Statute of the Inter-American Commission on Human Rights: (1) to make recommendations to the governments of member states on the adoption of measures fostering fundamental freedoms at the domestic level; (2) to prepare studies and reports on human rights; (3) to secure information from the governments on the measures adopted; and (4) to serve as advisory body in the area of human rights to the Organization of American States.

The Inter-American Convention of Human Rights has not been ratified by the United States. Although President Carter has announced that he will seek approval of the U.S. Senate for ratification, much remains to be done in the Inter-American System. The custom of Latin American governments to invoke the constitutional device known as the state of seige combined with repression by military dictatorships undermines human rights in the Western hemisphere.

Finally, such nongovernmental organizations (NGOs) as Amnesty International, the International League for Human Rights, the Minority Group, and others perform important investigative and communicative functions in the area of human rights. NGOs maintain a consultative status with the United Nations, its specialized agencies, and international conferences. The contributions of NGOs—including fact finding and monitoring and reporting human rights violations on the national and international level—are impressive. These agencies create a flow of information and exert pressure through lobbying in national states as well as international forums.

Western Context

The fundamental problem of political life—the tension between rights and duties of the individual and obligations and powers of the government—has characterized the development of the state. Since ancient Greece the West has approached this polarity within the framework of Platonic organicism and Sophistic nominalism. For the Platonists, the individual beyond a political community had no rights; it was through the polis that individuals gained the spiritual and political attributes which made them human, rather than barbarians. Therefore, concern for the whole of the political community preceded the claims of any individual. This type of political community was organic, since the individual functioned merely as a part of an organic whole and gained significance only in reference to that whole.

The Sophists, on the other hand, based the state upon a contract acknowledging that the individual had natural rights apart from the political community; the state arose only when individuals saw that it was to their interest to surrender their purely selfish interests in order to better secure them. For the Sophists the community was predicated upon a philosophy of nominalism; the members did have an identity beyond the political community. The rationale of the state was not to achieve an organic harmony and a common good, but rather to maximize the interests of the members of the state.

The Platonic-Sophistic dichotomy was reproduced with greater sophistication by the nominalists of the seventeenth century and the organicists of the nineteenth. Seventeenth century nominalism represented a final break with medieval organicism, which, following the dissemination of Aristotelian doctrines, provided the philosophical basis of political life in Europe. By the seventeenth century the community had become dissolved into a discrete mass of individuals with distinct self-interests. Hobbes built his state upon the selfishness of individuals; even Locke makes the individual enter political life for the benefits that accrue therefrom. Individuals left the "state of nature," in which life—Hobbes and Locke concurred—was "short, nasty, and brutish," through the social contract. The political community was then held together by an intricate balance of power which gave rise to a harmony of interests and became the basis of laissez faire economics and liberal politics. The interests of the individual and the community coincided.

The return to the organic notion of political community from seventeenth century nominalism took place in the works of Kant, Hegel, and Rousseau. Kant asserted that human values and perception were structured by objective categories which one brought into the world at birth. Accordingly, the individual had a categorical identity—a member of a class, nation, race—which ultimately determined one's actions. Rousseau substitutes the general will for the will of all. The difference between the will of all and the general will was that the latter had a transhistorical origin, which bore no necessary relationships to the interests of the members of the political community to which it applied. The will of all, on the other hand, was simply the will of the majority of the people. Finally, Hegel formalized the course of history. There was an absolute in history which dictated human action. Freedom was simply action in accord with historical necessity. Human values and human purpose were rendered operationally irrelevant by the inalterable course of history.

The transition from seventeenth century nominalism to nineteenth century organicism began with the reversion against the French Revolution and developed during the Industrial Revolution. With the emergence of the reign of virtuous terror in France, Europeans who had supported the original ideals of the Revolution recoiled to doctrines of organicism. The exponents of the new organicism—Burke, Demaistre, and Fichte—argued that political community was given by nature and could not be altered by political action. The values of the group to which the individual belonged were transhistorical. The course of history determined the significance of the group. Thus nineteenth century conservatives advanced the concept of the absolute. Burke found it in tradition, Fichte in the nation, Gobineau in the race, and Madison Grant in the aristocracy. Individuals' denial of a transcendent absolute, conservatives have imagined, has rendered them incapable of sustaining political order.

Even Marx, for instance, adopted all the trappings of nineteenth century organicism. The individual for him was born with an objective identity dictated by the division of labor, a corollary of the prevailing system of production which was a by-product of historical necessity. An eventual classless society was assured by the inalterable course of the historical absolute.

In the twentieth century the conservative longing has found its articulate and learned exponents. William Y. Elliot has written of the attack by pragmatism and pluralism on the absolute sovereignty of the constitutional state. Henry Kariel has lamented the twentieth century image of the political individual whose actions are environmentally determined and who is consequently incapable of positing transcendent political values. Richard M. Weaver, a consistent enemy of relativism, argues that the individual is dehumanized without the tyrannizing norms of culture.

The evidence of political life in the twentieth century, however, seems to refute the diagnosis of the conservatives. The paramount reality of twentieth century politics, the ''true believer,'' is distinguished precisely by a penchant to grasp an absolute through selfless dedication to the movement which embodies it. The selfless individual has appeared as the Bolshevik, the Nazi, the American, the Maoist. It is not the lack of absolutes, but the institutionalization of these absolutes, which has underscored the tension between the individual and the state.

The twentieth century lacks a public realm, as the classical Greeks understood it. The realm of freedom where individuals render their notions of the good political order has narrowed. The trend is toward ideological, "consensus" politics; membership in the political community of rights and duties is denied to those who remain beyond the pale of the prevailing dogma. In the absence of this realm of freedom, twentieth century man has been reduced to an instrument of necessity. Now, however, necessity appears in the guise of ideologies, surrogates of true political expression.

Thus the erosion of individual rights, the fruits of which were left for twentieth century individuals to bear, took place in the nineteenth century; Kant, Rousseau, and Hegel supplied the tools of the erosion. Freedom in the classical sense, in other words, has been the victim of the expression of nineteenth century attitudes and ideologies in the twentieth century political realm. The present crisis of human rights in the West is a function of ideological politics. The need for a new relationship between a freedom which recognizes a person's essential spiritual nature and an expanded necessity imposed by the nineteenth century heritage exerts strong pressure upon present society in the West.

The needs of the individual conflict with the demands of the nation-state which transformed the moral and political centers of authority, emasculating the political authority of the church and the family. It inherited many of the primary functions which these social organizations provided. Accordingly, in Western society human rights issues center around both the nature of the social structure and demands for new life-styles. The social structure of the state reflects the distribution of economic and political rewards among various competing interest and ethnic groups. Life-styles, on the other hand, refer to individuals who have grown dissatisfied with their roles and functions in society and the life-styles which they lead. They have developed new needs. The politics of life-styles involves very different consideration from the politics of social structure.

In such an environment clothing, preference in music or drugs, homosexuality or heterosexuality, become human rights issues. More specifically, individuals become more concerned with their self-determination and with the right for the private life. They want to preserve their individuality and what they consider important from the tyranny of atomization, automation, and alienation.

Marxist and Neo-Marxist Views

Marxism is an elaboration of the concept of humanism developed during the Renaissance asserting the basic dignity and worth of the individual and a person's capacity for self-realization through reason. Karl Marx emphasized economic rights, affirming that the collapse of the capitalist system was inevitable and that the proletariat (the working class) would seize the means of production and establish a new socialist system. This socialist system would then work toward the attainment of communism under which all would share equally the benefits of the new society. The exploited proletarian class would construct a new classless society where all individuals would be treated equally and justly.

The global character of Marxism has produced a diversity of opinion on the subject of Marxist humanism. In the Marxist societies (led by the Soviet Union), a more "traditional" approach to the subject of Marxist humanist thought has been emphasized. Traditional Marxist humanism focuses on class struggle and the liberation of the working class. The class struggle is the force that molds the consciousness of the working class and allows it to free itself from the oppression of the exploitative classes. As one traditional Marxist, Ladislav Shtoll, writes, "It will not be amiss to recall Engels' *The Condition of the Working Class in England* where it is stressed that the workers can maintain their human dignity, their human countenance, only if their whole life is filled with a burning hatred for the exploiter class."

The traditional Marxists contend that there is no genuine humanism under the capitalist system because of the oppressed condition of the working class. Under the capitalist system the worker is viewed only in terms of market value, not as a human being with a myriad of needs and cares. Thus, under such a system the basis for a humanist society could never be constructed. As another traditional Marxist writer, Roger Garaudy, phrased it, "The problems of humanism . . . are, in the final analysis, reduced to the need for a just organization of society."

While the traditional Marxists stress the class struggle and the monolithic unity of the communist movement, other Marxists are beginning to explore new routes to communism. These "neo-Marxists" are devoted to developing a more humane socialism independent of the present centers of Marxist thought in Moscow and Peking. The neo-Marxists are opposed to the harsh and repressive Stalinist system and demand autonomy for each national Marxist movement. The slogan of the neo-Marxists has been "Socialism with a human face." Leonard Wolfgang has observed, "Humanist Marxists reject the Soviet idea that a socialist society must be based on a planned state economy and be characterized by 'moral and political unity' under the leadership of an all-powerful party and its apparatus." Neo-Marxists view socialism as a free society based economically on the self-management of producers and characterized politically by democratic liberties and freedom of speech. Obviously many of these ideas contradict the Marxist-Leninist philosophy of a strong, centralized Communist party and the dictatorship of the proletariat as the method of government in a socialist state.

It is also significant that the neo-Marxists do not emphasize the class struggle. They are not exclusively concerned with changing the economic structures of society. Rather, the neo-Marxists stress democracy, freedom of discussion, and the problem of alienation. Michael Harrington observes, ''In communist society, alienation persists; indeed, it is writ large. The totalitarian state becomes the very incarnation of all those powers which weigh upon man, which rob him of his individuality and personality. There is anticapitalism, to be sure, but an anticapitalism which is corrosive of human dignity in much the same way as its antagonists.'' Harrington goes on to add, ''As soon as one realizes that socialism is not simply directed against economic irrationality but that its deepest springs flow from a positive humanism whose task is the conquest of alienation, it becomes obvious that Russian society has nothing to do with socialism.''

Neo-Marxist thought has risen to prominence in Western Europe (among the Eurocommunist parties) and in Tito's Yugoslavia, where exception from the Soviet model was taken in 1948. The neo-Marxist stress on democratic methods of governing and greater freedom could be interpreted as a reaction to the rigidity of Stalinism; it could also be viewed as the fear, on the part of other Communist parties, of being dominated by the Soviet Communist party. This fear is based on the historical experience of communism in Russia and of Soviet politics vis-à-vis Eastern Europe.

Following the death of Lenin, Stalin seized control of the party and purged many of the old Bolsheviks who disagreed with the party orthodoxy he set forth. Stalin followed a similar philosophy as Louis Antoine Saint-Just did following the French Revolution when he observed, ''A patriot is one who supports the republic as a whole; whoever resists it in detail is a traitor.'' As Maurice Merleau-Ponty puts it, ''Either this means nothing at all, or else it means that in a period of revolutionary tension or external threat there is no clear-cut boundary between political divergencies and objective treason. Humanism is suspended and government is Terror.''

Clearly the neo-Marxists wish to avoid such an occurrence in their theoretical path toward communism. The traditional Marxists reject the possibility of other paths to communism—that is, democratic elections versus violent revolution. They believe that only by changing the economic structure of society and economic relations between individuals can a new humanity be founded and a more humane society emerge. While neo-Marxists recognize that the economic structures must be changed to promote the new humanism, they emphasize values of individuality and freedom.

Third World

Existential conditions in the Third World differ considerably from those in the West. Increased institutionalization of the nation-state has accentuated the confrontations between the Western individual and the state. In the West human rights tensions derive from the frustrating efforts to fit the contemporary environment into the nation-state; tensions in the Third World represent their equally frustrating effort to fit the nation-state into their traditional institutions. Human rights concerns in the Third World center more around the nature of the social structure and less around life styles. Poverty, hunger, disease, illiteracy, low productivity, mass unemployment, glaring disparities in the distribution of benefits—all underscore the existential plight of the Third World.

The nation-state, and a progressive as opposed to a static vision of reality, have caused explorations, and sometimes conflagrations, in the relationships between traditional cultural patterns and the structures of government. The Third World is in a marked intellectual and political institutional discontinuity with the old. The family and the community have outlived their usefulness as organizing principles and as safeguards for certain basic human rights. Nothing has replaced them, except perhaps angry and sometimes ugly cynicism. Human rights in the Third World are thus in a stage of ferment. There is confusion and, at times, anarchy.

The nation-state model has required governments to enter into competition with traditional authority. This in turn has prompted the attempt to inject new values, interests, and goals in an effort to supplant those traditionally held or accepted. While the old has been destroyed, the new has not yet appeared. The reasons are technical as well as ideological. The new states have no commonly accepted values; hence their new national structures are easily perishable. Political systems in the Third World merge in the overriding context of Leninism and militarism with an everwidening public sector. Hardly any of the Third World governments has been able to institutionalize itself firmly, to establish liberal or popular institutions, or to relax its vigil against subversion, imagined or real. The central structures of government are modern in form only, not in substance. Government is minimal in organization and effect.

The purpose and functions of the state in most of the Third World differ from the Western model. The role of the state in Islam, for example, serves a useful illustration. Unlike the modern Western nation-state, the Islamic state is obliged to enforce principles of the Shariah (Islamic law) in the territory under its jurisdiction. The implementation of the Shariah means inter alia that the Islamic state must create an environment conducive to the socioreligious needs of the people. Another salient difference between the Western nation-state and the Islamic state is that in the latter's case sovereignty belongs to God alone. Both the rulers and the ruled are working for the glory of God whose wishes and commands must be fulfilled for achieving happiness here and in the hereafter. Since sovereignty belongs to God alone, the process of legislation becomes less significant in an Islamic state than it is in its counterpart in the West.

God has created human beings who seek perfection, following the perfected and mastership of the will. Human beings have certain God-granted rights, and right by definition is the exercise of power. Islam defines the behavior of individuals as well as the society at large. The integrity of the self, which is tantamount to human dignity, is God granted and is realized through human wisdom serving the good of the society as a whole. Society is based on production to take care of the needs of its members. The requirement for the regulation of production creates the political system, an organization that would regulate and direct—as well as create—just and applicable laws. The Islamic political system seeks harmony for itself, its units, and its environment. The duty of the individual to defend the system is balanced by the obligation of the system to satisfy the needs of its members. Thus the system is based upon self-sufficiency.

If we accept the opinion that the Shariah, which is derived from the Quran, is the raison d'etre of the Islamic state, then we are obliged to accept the argument that it is the state's duty to enhance human dignity and alleviate conditions that hinder individuals in their effort to achieve happiness. However, in practice Islamic legal theory provides no adequate machinery to safeguard individual rights against the state. Modern Turkey has dealt with this problem by establishing a system of guaranteed individual liberties in the secularization of the state. Pakistan, on the other hand, has sought to establish a system of individual rights through a liberal interpretation of the original sources of Islamic law. The vast majority of the other Islamic states have adopted Western concepts of individual rights. Only Saudi Arabia applies the Shariah fully.

The record of human rights in modern Turkey is relatively better than in most of the other Islamic states. Pakistan, on the other hand, has been beset by domestic strife depriving it of the opportunity to test its system of individual rights. In the Islamic states that have patterned their political systems after Western or Marxist models, there is constant confrontation between individual rights and obligations and state duties and powers. In Saudi Arabia, where the Shariah has been applied without interruption since the seventh century, rights are enjoyed within the context of Islamic values and denied to those who remain beyond the prevailing dogma. Put differently, the only rights enjoyed are those prescribed by the original sources of Islamic law.

Environmental changes in the Third World have outstripped the institutional structures of the traditional era. The promise of higher stages of material growth competes with the negative conditions of underdeveloped existence to push down human rights priorities. The collision of old values, new concepts, and foreign exploitation underlies the problem of modernization and development.

Third World states are attempting to telescope the achievements of the industrial revolution into one generation. Their people have discovered themselves in unfamiliar ways. They are forced to choose between affecting change within their political system or renouncing the relevance of their values to their present existence. Since they cannot do the latter, they must choose the former. This is a period of maximum transition in the Third World, in contrast to the previous three hundred years when it remained much outside the political forces operating in the West. The pressure of new ideas is explosive. While receptiveness to new ideas is strong, reluctance to let go of older ones is still greater.

The processes of change have blurred the distinction between modernization and development. The development process is the way the potential for society and its members is sought. It is a process with a goal—even if this goal is perceived as an ever receding one. True, there is always a utopia by which the development process is measured. Utopias are extracted from a people's experience and generalized into a vision of the desired society. But since experience is constantly enlarged, it is natural that the utopia changes. How a person manages the tension between theory and practice, reflection and experience,—this proxiological style helps keep the dreams alive. Otherwise the dream becomes a nightmare.

Modernization is the adoption of modern technology for the increase of productivity. In the Third World societal values are not integrated into the emerging designs of development. Modernization is not a substitute for development. What is occurring in the less developed countries is that development is simply latched on to modernization because no other popular base is constructed.

The vitality of the vision of development can derive only from its cultural reality, neither from Western liberalism nor from the variety of Marxist experiences. Human rights in the Third World are sacrificed for modernization. Regardless of time and place, individuals must sweat out their own development to the greater expansion of their dignity.

World Order

The entire global system today is gripped by frustrations and crises. At first glance, it appears as if the rapprochement of the superpowers has produced peace. In fact, the superpowers' reconciliation purchases minimal security in exchange for vital interests of the less developed countries. Already exponents of a new world order are asserting that the new detente of the superpowers (the United States, the USSR, and the People's Republic of China), demonstrates superpower indifference toward the rapidly growing gap between the rich and powerful states and an indifference to the humanist ideals of peace and equality that were framed in the declarations and convenants on human rights.

As Brady Tyson has remarked, rather than a liberal, democratic, egalitarian order of law to replace the anarchy of the nation-state system, an international corporatist order appears to be developing, which is neither liberal nor democratic. A corporatist system is one where interest groups are represented by their elite in concert with other interest group elites, and the concert of elites develops its own interest while maintaining control over their respective groups. That is, the heads of several interest groups (the army, big business, and banks) form an alliance to preserve stability in their common universe and to create stability, and thereby virtually eliminate or severely limit competition among the groups they head.

The security managers of the three superpowers, in pursuit of their respective interests, form an informal network of understanding and communication to assure that competition among them will not be allowed to become destructive, and that potential rivals will be contained before they can threaten the dominance of the big three or any one of them. It is sort of an international cartel for the restraint of competition, and to limit the power to change the rules of the game to the three major actors. And, of course, there is no international antitrust legislation of any significance.

The three superpowers are now tacitly aligned against a change in favor of the poor and weak states—and the old colonial policy of divide and rule characterizes the relations between them and the smaller states. The superpowers are serving notice on the rest of the world that they will not be maneuvered into confrontation by the other states. Undoubtedly, the period when the superpowers could be played off against each other has come to an end. The tendency henceforth will be for the superpowers to negotiate directly among themselves, and treat their clients as such.

From the standpoint of world development, it is tragic that the period of superpower conflict was very often used to enhance the prosperity of the superpowers and militarize rather than develop the Third World. The era of the emerging rapprochement may tend to deescalate the international military conflicts in the Third World, but it is not likely—on the other hand—to increase development assistance from the rich to the poor states. For one thing, the development process tends to be destabilizing, and that is apparently not a goal of any of the superpowers at this time.

Thus the inevitable tendency in such a three-superpower arrangement will be to reduce the area of maneuver of the less developed countries, and to maintain or force them into client relations with one of the superpowers. Military modernizers who will avoid exciting "extravagant" popular expectations such as those in the Universal Declaration of Human Rights will probably continue to appear and flourish in the Third World, sponsored by one or the other of the superpowers.

In his work on human rights, Brady Tyson has compared the 1930s to the 1970s. Like the thirties, the seventies are times of severe testing of liberalism and constitutionalism. In both cases the reasons are near identical: social dislocations caused by unplanning and unregulated changes provoked by technological change, national and corporate competition, and power—and profit hunger. Liberalism and constitutionalism have easily become the prisoners of their own traditional processes, and have failed to keep up with the necessity to adapt to new conditions. In the 1930s the challenge of international communism created a counterrevolution from the Right, which was only contained by World War II. In the 1970s the challenge of protest movements without a program have been taken advantage of by a counterrevolution (the "New Right") that is yet to be contained.

While the global political system is dominated by corporatism, the global economic system assumes the form of industrial feudalism. The present global system consists of no more than about twenty-five states and fifty multinational corporations who have any significant impact, and the top five states have over half of the world's human and natural resources.

The United States, with a GNP of nearly $2 trillion, nearly 40 percent of the world's industrial production, and 75 percent of its computer capacity, raises the issue of who has the rights to world resources. America's power is increasingly exercised by a pluralistic, diffuse, and differentiated elite, residing throughout the world but increasingly Americanized in style and outlook. Today the United States occupies a position similar to Rome during the Middle Ages: a nominal center of power forced to exercise influence through indirect diffused means and multinational corporations. The industrial states constitute less than a fourth of world population and enjoy more than three-fourths of its annual GNP. The United States, with 7.5 percent of the world population, controls more than one-fourth of world GNP and consumes 30 percent of the nonrenewable resources produced each year (including 37 percent of the energy, 25 percent of the steel, 28 percent of the tin, and 28 percent of the synthetic rubber). In the Third World about 750 million people lack minimal requirements of food, medical care, housing, and literacy. More than one billion people in the Third World earn less than $150 a year.

Several of the multinational corporations (such as Royal Dutch/Shell, Standard Oil, Texaco, Mobil, Gulf, and IBM) exert more collective influence than all but a handful of states, principally the industrial ones. The pattern of investment and activity of these corporations affects issues of war and peace and determines the long-term prospects for world economic development and allocation of world resources. Decision making by these companies has as much or more impact on human conditions and international conflict and cooperation as do the foreign policy decisions of states as Brazil, Iran, or the Phillippines.

This maldistribution of wealth is accompanied by a maldistribution of information. The same industrial states and multinational corporations also enjoy the political and economic control over the international exchange of information. The advanced industrial states have come to rely less and less on such markets as extractive industries and are bound together in a fierce competition to secure new technologies to maintain their superiority. With the abatement of unregulated competition among the superpowers, the appeals and publicity about the plight of the Third World, about hunger, poverty, and underdevelopment, will probably die down. But given the continuing population growth, and the capital- and technology-intensive nature of the usual postindustrial modernization process, these problems are hardly likely to diminish. In the face of the new

situation the United Nations and the international agencies can hardly be
expected to maintain even their present low level of impact, since these
agencies exist—or act by the sufferance of—the major powers in key issues.

American Foreign Policy

The last quarter of the twentieth century has dramatized the issue of human
rights in American foreign policy. In his Inaugural Address President Carter
underscored the importance of a U.S. committment to and respect for human
rights. The human rights initiatives of the Carter administration, however, have
produced both support and criticism. Opponents wonder whether it is realistic
to emphasize human rights in a U.S. foreign policy which deals with sovereign
states and whose purpose is to promote national interest and safeguard national
security. They assert that the United States cannot apply a single human rights
standard to all states regardless of levels of development and degree of friend-
ship with the United States. They argue that it is not correct for the United States
to be the moral arbiter for a world where Western concepts of human rights
differ markedly from the human rights priorities of other cultures. Exponents of
the Carter initiatives, however, assert that violations in some countries are
excessive and threaten such basic human needs that they transcend cultural and
political differences among states. They emphasize that without ensuring
minimum survival for every citizen of the globe, the rights that Americans
cherish become endangered.

The American foreign policy posture on human rights has been preceded by
congressional involvement through both legislative and investigative functions. (The discussion on the rule of Congress and the president in the area of
human rights is based upon *Human Rights and U.S. Foreign Policy*, Washington, D.C.: Congressional Research Service, 1977, authored by Vita Bite.)
Congress has passed legislation to limit the provision of assistance to countries
in particular circumstances. The Foreign Assistance Acts of 1973 and 1974
both included sections linking the receipt of foreign assistance to the protection
of human rights. Section 32 of the act of 1973 provided that

> the President should deny any economic or military assistance to the
> government of any foreign country which practices the internment or
> imprisonment of that country's citizens for political purpose.

Section 46 of the act of 1974 requires the president to reduce or terminate
security assistance to any government which consistently violates internationally recognized human rights. Violations of human rights were specified as

> including torture or cruel, inhuman or degrading treatment or punish-
> ment; prolonged detention without charges; or other flagrant denials of
> the right to life, liberty and the security of the person.

Congress also enacted human rights legislation directed at specific countries.
In 1974 Congress limited military assistance to Korea for fiscal year 1974

"until the President submits a report to the Congress . . . stating that the government of South Korea is making substantial progress in the observance of internationally recognized standards of human rights." Congressional appropriations for assistance to Chile were prohibited or limited by Congress to express its concern over human rights in that country. Congress also enacted legislation aimed at addressing human rights in the Soviet Union and Eastern Europe. Congress stipulated that no funds were to be used to provide military assistance, international military education and training, or foreign military credit sales to Uruguay.

The International Development and Food Assistance Act of 1975 utilizes language that appears frequently in resolutions of the United Nations: "Consistent pattern of gross violations of internationally recognized human rights." That same act provides that economic assistance may not be given to any country which consistently violates human rights; requires the president to submit to Congress a report explaining how assistance would benefit directly the people of such a country; and stipulates that if either house of Congress disagrees with the president's justification, it may terminate economic assistance to that country.

The International Security Assistance and Arms Exportation Control Act of 1976 also utilizes standards and criteria that have been established by the United Nations. This act declares that it "is the policy of the United States . . . to promote and encourage increased respect for human rights and fundamental freedoms for all . . . . To this end, a principal goal of the foreign policy of the United States is to promote the increased observance of internationally recognized human rights by all countries." That same act established a coordinator for human rights and humanitarian affairs in the Department of State and required the secretary of state to submit annual reports on human rights in countries receiving security assistance. In 1977 the Department of State established a new Bureau of Human Rights and Humanitarian Affairs.

In 1976 the U.S. Congress also adopted legislation requiring the U.S. executive directors of the Inter-American Development Bank and the African Development Fund "to vote against any loan, any extension of financial assistance, or any technical assistance to any country which engages in a consistent pattern of gross violations of internationally recognized human rights, including torture or cruel, inhumane, or degrading treatment or punishment, prolonged detention without charges, or other flagrant denials of the right to life, liberty, and the security of person, unless such assistance will directly benefit the needy people in such country."

In his March 17, 1977 speech at the United Nations, President Carter called for strengthening of the UN Human Rights Commission and for the implementation of a twelve-year-old proposal for the establishment of an independent UN commissioner for human rights. He also declared his intention to seek approval for U.S. ratification of four UN human rights instruments—the Covenant on Civil and Political Rights, the Covenant on Economic, Social, and Cultural

Rights, the UN Genocide Convention and the Convention on the Elimination of All Forms of Racial Discrimination.

Recent administration actions and statements on human rights seem to reflect a more cautious position than was the case earlier. On April 6, 1977 the House of Representatives agreed to two human rights amendments authorizing U.S. contributions to international lending institutions. The first required U.S. officials of all international financial institutions to vote against extending financial assistance to any member state found to have a consistent pattern of gross violations of human rights. The second required the secretaries of state and treasury to negotiate with other states to develop viable standards for meeting basic human needs and protecting human rights. The first amendment was agreed to despite the opposition of President Carter, who describes such an approach to human rights as ''at once too lenient and too rigid.'' The president had favored an amendment which encouraged (but did not require) American representatives to international financial organizations to seek to channel loans to countries other than those engaging in a consistent pattern of gross violations of internationally recognized human rights. On April 20, 1977 the Senate Foreign Relations Committee agreed with the president's position not requiring automatic rejection of aid to nations found violating human rights.

More recently, Secretary of State Cyrus Vance has emphasized limits on U.S. action in this area. In a speech on April 30, 1977 Secretary of State Vance, while restating the U.S. commitment to human rights, explained that the promotion of human rights must be realistic, and must not include imposition of American values on others. He noted that there are constraints on U.S. policy in this area and that American policy should be determined flexibly on a country-by-country basis. Secretary Vance specified human rights as consisting of three parts—integrity of the individual, fulfillment of basic human needs, and civil and political liberties.

Human rights is also an issue in Soviet-American relations because each side views and acts upon the matter from conflicting ideological perspectives. The American-Soviet human rights debate rests upon the Final Act of the Conference on Security and Cooperation in Europe, signed at Helsinki in 1975. The document is not legally binding, but rather represents a statement of principles which reaffirms the purposes and principles of the Universal Declaration of Human Rights.

The issue of human rights presents a problem of priority for the United States. The American government must reconcile between human rights and arms control as important issues in U.S. foreign policy toward the Soviet Union. The Soviets may succeed in suppressing the dissident movement and contain its spread into Eastern Europe. While such an outcome would be disturbing to the United States, it could minimize Soviet objections, and render the SALT negotiations more manageable.

Competing Foci

There are many views of human rights, but hardly a clear focus. Human rights in the West are expressed in demands for the redress of grievances and for the satisfaction of new needs, while in the past they represented a desire to be left alone. The Greco-Roman and the Judeo-Christian traditions asserted both rights and duties, as expounded in the "natural law" arguments of the times.

Thus in the West we see a movement away from the individual's obligations to the state in favor of demands that the state perform more duties. As each stage develops, the number of individual rights expands while the province of individual obligations narrows. On the other hand, the demand for the expansion of the duties of the state is satisfied only through the enlargement of state powers. These contradictory aspects run deep in the present human rights debate in the West. This contradiction has placed the state in cross fire between individuals and groups demanding equal rights. The essential contradiction is that government intervention to meet demands of an individual or a group decreases the rights of other individuals or groups in exact proportion to its success. The trend will persist until such time when there occurs a change in the allocation of power.

We must also recognize the connection between the type and number of rights and the nature of the environment. In the West there has been a definite shift from an abstract concept of universal rights toward a concrete concept of essential rights. The shift is indicative of societal conditions that must be taken into consideration in the dialogue on human rights. The West is in a stage of development substantially different from much of the Third World. The problems associated with Third World development have not been experienced in the recent history of the West.

In the Third World human rights focus upon such essentials as hunger, inadequate sanitation, and lack of shelter. In the meantime, protagonists of change in the less developed countries suffer indignities of torture and political imprisonment. Their demand for human rights continues to expand. Eventually the Third World will experience a cycle of evolution of human rights similar to that of the West, but in reverse order—from concrete essential rights to abstract universal rights to concrete rights again. In the process certain human rights conflict in specific circumstances, the reasons for the differences in particular lists of rights being both historical and functional. The need for trade-offs between the ideal and the possible forces the Third World to assign priorities. However, it is not too early for the Third World to assess the price of modernization. It is imperative to ask which value will cost the least.

Responding to Challenge

The United States, with a GNP nearing $2 trillion, enjoys leadership responsibilities to meet the challenges of human rights, both domestically and internationally. The domestication of international politics and the internationalization of domestic politics gives the struggle for human rights global affinity. The human need for a sense of community transcends the barriers of geography that separate American affluence from Third World poverty. The glib talk of incinerating continents should be traded for global reform.

America is still a moral exemplar to the world. There is no inherent contradiction between power and morality. Power becomes destructive only when committed to the service of a narrow conception of morality. Power may be used for moral or immoral purposes. U.S. power provides the possibilities to overcome the despair of the Third World or the mindless optimism of advocates of technocratic images of the future. American power can serve such foreign policy goals as the development of harmonious interaction between the individual and nature and the promotion of human solidarity. Lack of moral absolutes to world politics does not free us from our responsibility to remain human beings.

The issue confronting U.S. foreign policy is not intervention versus nonintervention. The commitment to human rights requires a foreign policy process to promote them. It is the style of American intervention that is at issue. What is required is dignity that corresponds to our stature. This entails a posture where U.S. foreign policy reflects its observed rank among states. A powerful and rich country is not obsessed with the politics of scarcity in dealings with the world. Only small and poor states are motivated by survival, and rightly so. A great country deals with great crises. The political viability of humanity, not of a political regime, must be a criterion of American commitment. The ecology of the planet, not shrimp beds off a remote coast, must be the focus of American interest. America enjoys a broad spectrum of action appropriate to its commitment. Otherwise Americans dedicate their foreign policy to the noble purpose of making ends meet.

The base of any foreign policy is a state's mission to maximize its value synthesis. The inclusion of human rights among American foreign policy values requires a sophistication that is beyond the rightful idealism of some of us or the cold cynicism of others. A national interest narrowly defined and external threats vastly exaggerated create a poor foreign policy vision. Only we are reasonably satisfied in the security of our national interest and therefore can perceive direct relationship between self-interest and a dignified world order. If it is the task of the state to survive, those who ponder security problems should not become enamored with their options. This must be so because security is as much a state of mind as it is a physical condition.

The American hard talk about human rights is not a substitute for acting hard. The boundary of sacrifice does not stop at the American shores. When we adjust our domestic growth and share our international growth with the less developed countries, we join the partnership of human rights. The foreign assistance legislation enacted by the Congress in 1973 and 1974, the International Development and Food Assistance Act of 1975, and the International Security Assistance and Arms Export Act of 1976 mark the road for new directions in U.S. foreign policy. The footsteps of present-day Americans could become the trodden path of human dignity.□

READINGS SUGGESTED BY THE AUTHOR:

Bite, Vita. *Human Rights and U.S. Foreign Policy*. Washington, D.C.: Congressional Research Service, 1977.

Castberg, Frede. *The European Convention on Human Rights*. Oceana, 1974.

Claude, Richard P. *Comparative Human Rights*. Baltimore: Johns Hopkins University Press, 1976.

del Russo, Allessandra L., International Protection of Human Rights. Washington, D.C.: Lerner Law Book Company, 1971.

Emerson, R. "The Fate of Human Rights in the Third World," *World Politics* 27 (January 1975): 201-26.

Garaudy, Roger. *Marxist Humanism*. Paris: Edition Sociales, 1957.

Harrington, Michael. "Marx as Humanist," in Michael Curtis, ed., *Marxism*. New York: Atherton, 1970.

Leonhard, Wolfgang. *Three Faces of Marxism*. New York: Holt, Rinehart & Winston, 1974.

Machan, Tibor R. *Human Rights and Human Liberties: A Radical Reconsideration of the American Political Tradition*. Chicago: Nelson-Hall, 1975.

Merleau-Ponty, Maurice. *Humanism and Terror*. Boston: Beacon Press, 1971.

Shtoll, Ladislav. "The Class Struggle and Humanism," *World Marxist Review*. Vol. 1, no. 3, 1958.

Van Dyke, Vernon. *Human Rights, The United States and World Community*. New York: Oxford University Press, 1970.

PROSPECTS FOR HUMAN RIGHTS

DAVID RIESMAN
Harvard University

The current American campaign for human rights contains a serious ethnocentric bias. I should make clear, however, that I myself am not free of biases; I can only strive to be aware of them. For only through discussion can biases be brought to light and ambiguities clarified; only through discussion can I learn where I have been mistaken, where I have been misunderstood.

Human Rights

The concepts of human rights and human prospects suggest the possibility of conflicts among our ideals, that is, the possibility that the proclaimed goal of human rights may inadvertently risk the human prospects of survival itself. This is the risk of immediate destruction through what I have regarded, since Hiroshima, as the overarching danger to the species: the existence of nuclear weapons and the possibility to which these give rise of an escalating nuclear conflict among the superpowers. I supported the candidacy of President Carter on a number of grounds, chief among them the fact that he is the first president with a technical understanding of those weapons and with a serious and systematic interest in controlling and eventually banishing them—an effort that must begin between the Soviet Union and ourselves before we can hope to restrain proliferation among those other nations who now possess such weapons in actuality or potential.

At the same time, in lending his prestige and immense moral capital to the campaign for human rights vis-à-vis the Soviet Union, it is possible that President Carter has jeopardized his hopes on the all-important nuclear front, not only because prominent officialdom in the Soviet Union says so, but because of the long-run impact of the Carter campaign on *American* public opinion. Indeed, it is difficult to predict the possible impact of the human rights campaign, not so much on the vocal dissidents who have already suffered jeopardy, but on the generally silent but nonetheless in the long run influential public opinion of nonelites in the Soviet Union and its uneasy satellites.

The campaign for human rights vis-à-vis the Soviet Union of course did not begin with President Carter. In one sense it goes back to the very beginning of the Soviet regime, while long before that the insistence of many Americans on the proper moral conduct of other countries was a factor in launching us both into the Spanish-American War and the First World War. The contemporary campaign vis-à-vis the Soviet Union would seem to take its origin at the conclusion of the fighting in Vietnam, and, in some degree, to represent the unliquidated continuation of the American domestic conflict over that war by other means and with somewhat altered partisans.

Liberal intellectuals, public officials, and interest groups ranging from influential American Zionists to longshoremen to the hard-liners who run the international division of the AFL-CIO have been in the forefront of the human rights issue, in some part as an attack on the efforts to achieve détente by former President Nixon and Henry Kissinger—an attack joined by the Republican Cold War Right, and the Democratic-liberal Left with its call for an open moral diplomacy, superior to realpolitik. The campaign appeals to our idealism: to our hope of living in a world without torture, without slavery, one where people are free to speak and to move about—although the current campaign against illegal immigrants and, indeed, against any further immigration at all fits in badly with a desire for more open frontiers.

It is not sufficient argument against our human rights campaign that we ourselves often violate our own ideals in practice, not only vis-à-vis immigration of people but also vis-à-vis importation of goods which others can make more efficiently than we and which we attempt to limit or keep out through ever increasing efforts at protectionism. The very point of an ideal is that it is something not easily achieved. And no American policy, foreign or domestic, is viable which rests on a definition of the national interest—a questionable concept—which fails to take account of our national idealism; the problem is to adjudicate among competing ideals.

The notion that ideals may not be compatible with each other is often difficult for Americans to accept; we are inclined to believe that all good things are compatible, that we can have *both* human survival and human rights without any risk to the former or compromise or delay with respect to the latter. This resembles the belief that we can have more jobs *and* more environmental amenities, more social and human services *and* less strenuous and exhausting conditions in the work to be done. Furthermore, the focus on human rights, though now voiced by a generally liberal Democratic administration, inevitably plays into the never wholly defeated Cold War mentality of ethnocentric and patrioteering Americans even while President Carter is seeking to open up our relations with Cuba and Panama, with Vietnam and even with North Korea.

Nuclear Threat

The current generation of young people has not grown up with nightmares of the possibility of nuclear devastation. Vietnam was not seen as an issue of nuclear peril, as it was for me, but as a moral outrage and, for many, a personal threat and a personal moral dilemma. Since we have lived for over thirty years without the use of nuclear weapons in war, our good fortune in this respect reminds me of Joseph Schumpeter's verdict on capitalism: it would be destroyed by its beneficiaries who had no hand in its adventures and triumphs. Similarly, those who have not had to deal with the detailed issues (for example, of the current SALT agreements and all previous arms control negotiations) are the beneficiaries of an unearned beneficence which directs their idealism toward other, readier targets—for example, the Seabrook power plant.

My generation is the product of a different history. I did not share a number of attitudes that prevailed in this country during the Second World War. I never for a moment had any sympathy for Stalinism, and I regarded Soviet brutalities as quite as murderous as Hitler's. Yet, despite my fear lest Hitler emerge victorious, I believed at the time and still do that the British and American bombing of Dresden and Hamburg, as well as Tokyo and other large Japanese cities, transcended the limits which need to be placed on warfare and was not necessary for Allied survival, since for those who would listen there was evidence that the Japanese were succumbing to a naval blockade and that the emperor and his circle were eager for peace. Vis-à-vis the Nazis, if we had not demanded unconditional surrender, we might not have had to wage total war with such destructive weapons. Only in the Vietnam War did any large number of educated Americans begin to criticize the waging of total war against civilian populations even with the excuse of saving American lives when the cost was the destruction of civilian "enemy" life (including plant life in Vietnam) in the country under attack.

Still, terrible as these mass bombings were, carried on with so-called conventional weapons, the use of nuclear bombs at Hiroshima and Nagasaki marked a profound dividing line. In the decades since then I have fought those supposed realists like Edward Teller and many strategists who, pointing out that the largest conventional weapons were more deadly than the smallest nuclear ones, sought to erase the formal line between nuclear war and all other kinds of war. The idea, toyed with in Vietnam, that one could use tactical nuclear weapons, seemed a dangerous delusion; things generally go wrong with such calculations, and escalation to mutual annihilation could be the likely result.

Soviet-American Rapprochement

There have been many agonizing moments over the last thirty years in which hopes for rapprochement were shattered by internal politics of the Soviet Union or of the United States. Or just as a meeting was planned to discuss the end of nuclear testing, and the possibility of controlling nuclear weapons, something accidental prevented it—for example, the U-2 spy flight (which may not have been accidental, but undertaken by those who wanted to risk and perhaps torpedo the forthcoming summit meeting between Khrushchev and Eisenhower). In this context President Carter's raising of the human rights issue at the same time that he hoped to assure success of the SALT talks gives a feeling of déjà vu.

Tribalism within nation-states and among nation-states remains the most powerful force at work in the world today, more powerful even than class conflicts although especially powerful when tribal and class divisions coincide. The recent American presidential election was fought along both lines of fission. When I became an early supporter of candidate Jimmy Carter, I found myself opposed by many on the grounds of both regional and religious tribalism—by people with no understanding of or sympathy with the complexities of southern theological traditions and suspicious of white southerners in general. Yet as C. Vann Woodward pointed out a number of years ago, white southerners are the only major American group to have suffered military defeat, and at least in some instances are therefore likely to have a sense of limits and of tragedy. This has not been a general American characteristic, not even a southern one.

But President Carter is as American as he is southern. He has an all-American faith that problems are soluble and that they can be resolved not only within but among nations, especially when talked about candidly and openly. Candor can be both right conduct and successful strategy. Yet to believe that it will always work seems to me an often unconscious ethnocentric failure to appreciate that we cannot approach other countries in the same way that at times, in our cults of intimacy and of sharing, in our demolishing of the line between public and private, we approach each other both in adversary journalism and in many aspects of personal life.

The fact that the Soviet Union lacks adversary journalism (except in *Samizdat* or the privately circulated writings of dissidents) and is not an open society has been a stumbling block in the efforts to secure a test ban treaty which would cover underground testing, since our negotiators insisted at the time of the negotiation of the 1963 partial test ban treaty that it would be impossible without such inspection to distinguish between an underground test and an earthquake. This was a mistaken and even tendentious judgment: the best seismic experts believe that a distinction is easily made between an underground test and an earthquake; moreover, our spy satellites and our intelligence can tell us what is going on in the Soviet Union, even though we do not always want to reveal how much we know because that will tip off the Soviet Union as to how we know it. Above all, any analysis of this sort must distinguish between capabilities and intentions, and much of our thinking about the Soviet Union, like that of military men professionally, has been "worst case" thinking—a mode of thinking which can be self-confirming since it creates an alliance of the supposedly patriotic war party inside the United States with the patriotic war party within the Soviet Union, against the civilian populations of both countries.

Again to underline the fact that Jimmy Carter did not begin but is in fact trying to curb the American temptation to worst case thinking, we should recall the fact that candidate John Kennedy made the utterly factitious "missile gap" the main theme of his attack on candidate Richard Nixon and the previous Republican administration—indeed, later, at the time of the Cuban missile crisis, he did what no other American president has done: endangered the planet in order to force Premier Khruschev to back down. He created a crisis situation out of the Soviet missiles in Cuba, an issue that could have been handled more safely over time, since in reality the United States was no more threatened by these' missiles in Cuba (over which Soviet control was maintained) than by those ICBMs already in place or potentially located in offshore submarines. The relatively conciliatory Khrushchev, who had been the first openly to admit to the crimes of the Stalin era, was forced out of office by his internal enemies, in part as a result of this. But in the finest act of his presidency, John Kennedy got the Joint Chiefs of Staff and other crucial "hard-line" groups not to oppose the partial test ban treaty of 1963 even though he was unable to achieve a ban on all tests, in the atmosphere and underground.

Perilous Campaign

The history of our relations with the Soviet Union over the control of nuclear weapons is a history of might-have-beens. When President Eisenhower, in what was for him an uncharacteristic act of boyish openness, accepted responsibility for the U-2 overflight, one possible moment of rapprochement was lost. Now Brezhnev may be forced out of office by his illness, giving still further power to other factions in the Soviet military-industrial complex, before a new SALT agreement has been reached.

It is in this situation that the launching of the human rights campaign against the Soviet Union seems so perilous. It was not begun by candidate or President Carter. It has been carried on by Senator Jackson and others in the Senate—and Senator Jackson is a man who, contrary to widespread cynicism, is not only the "Senator from Boeing Aircraft," but also a true believer in human rights, as are many other idealistic Americans. And just as Senator Jackson had been mistaken in insisting that the Soviet Union would on materialistic grounds accept our trade terms while accepting also our vocal criticism concerning the emigration of Jewish dissidents (we raised no question about other captive nationalities), so President Carter began his administration by insisting that the Soviet Union would come to terms on the SALT agreements (and also on other outstanding issues) because there would be gains for it, and at the same time insisting on its accepting our standards of human rights as well.

Meantime, the Senate has already indicated where it stands by its vote of considerably less than two-thirds in favor of the confirmation of Paul Warnke as our disarmament negotiator. And the human rights issue itself vis-à-vis the Soviet Union can be taken up readily by the Congress to use against the president, who is himself now inclined to be more cautious on the issue—in other words, to use against a SALT agreement, restricting the development of new nuclear weapons systems. In fact, the judgment of many experts is that we are more than amply protected by the mobile and dispersed weapons we already possess. By giving the movement for human rights full legitimacy at an earlier point, it may have transcended President Carter's ability to control and focus it.

Soviet Politics

But I now must enter an area where I can claim no expertise: that of the internal politics of the Soviet Union—yet an area where I am guided by a certain skepticism bred by experience with American Sovietologists going back to the 1930s. I had the odd experience, during the height of the Cold War in the middle and late 1950s, of being told that I was "soft on communism" by people whom I had known when they were Communists, Trotskyites, Schachtmanites, and so on, and when I was, as I have remained, convinced of the brutality, corruption, and—in many areas—sheer incompetence of Soviet society. Some of these Russian experts were among the last to realize what Victor Zorza had long been pointing out: the likelihood of a Sino-Soviet split in what had been thought of as monolithic world communism. More important, the Soviet Union suffers even more from internal tribalism than we do, with many nationalities struggling to get out from under the control of the Great Russians, and in which the countries of the Eastern zone produce superior consumer goods and have a higher standard of living, despite having constantly to pay tribute to the Soviet Union, than do the citizens of the latter.

I am not contending that Soviet citizens are ready to break out in open revolt, but rather that Soviet authorities see themselves as beleaguered by China on the west, West Germany and the especially threatening dangers of French and Italian communism in Western Europe (threatening because they are not under Soviet hegemony), and then of course by the United States. The Soviet Union has never been able to achieve the kind of disciplined work force and the internalized as well as superficial obedience that the Chinese Communists appear to have been able to instill, drawing in part on long Confucian and other traditions. Hence, the fact that the Soviets have a long tradition of superiority in artillery, and that they can make and no doubt deliver huge bombs, is as much a sign of defensiveness as agression—indeed, their foreign policy in recent years has brought a series of defeats—even though their defensiveness, in dialectic with ours, may, in the form of nuclear war, end their prospects and ours.

This outlook has meant (for me, at least) a necessary restraint in criticism of the Soviet Union, even while prior to today's era there remained in this country quite a few influential intellectuals and writers who, as currently in many European countries, blinded themselves to the cruelties of the regime because it called itself socialist and because of their awareness of the evils of their own nation-states. And today I am in a position of deep moral ambiguity because, on the one hand, I admire enormously the courage of the Soviet dissidents, whatever their personal ideologies, and share many of the values that inspire someone like the scientist Sakharov; but at the same time I have consistently refused to sign petitions or in any other way lend my name to the criticisms of the treatment of these dissidents. In a bipolar nuclear world we cannot afford to hold to a simple, straightforward, universalistic moral standard such as one might hope for in a world free of the threat of mass annihilation.

There are many students of the Soviet Union who would disagree with my analysis, who believe that the regime is fully effective, secure, and un-threatened, that its leaders only pretend to be stung by criticisms—criticisms which are justified in any circumstances other than our nuclear era at the very moment when we are trying to reach across that chasm for some understanding. Thus my position on human rights does not spring from cultural or moral relativism. While one must take account of local conditions, and of the perils and priorities of other peoples, that does not mean that one condones ancient Aztec human sacrifice or today's tribal murders in Bangladesh. To repeat: it is because I see the nuclear question as always foremost that I cannot be sanguine about the human prospect in the long run, unless the human rights issue of this moment in this country is made less salient.

Human Prospects

This brings me to a second theme, that of human prospects. My phrase is in part an allusion to a small book by Robert Heilbroner, entitled *An Inquiry into the Human Prospect*. It deals with familiar issues, particularly the problems of pollution and overpopulation. I emphasize Heilbroner's work because it is that of a political economist, rather than of an environmentalist, ecologist, or demographer, and I share his preoccupations.

A decade or so ago I served on the Commission on National Goals of the National Planning Association; we concluded that even if we could shift large resources from defense expenditures to domestic priorities, and even if we taxed the well-to-do more heavily, there would never be enough to go around to satisfy the expectations and entitlements we had already agreed upon within our own country, whether in health care or protection for the elderly or in other social services. And all this was before the escalating costs of the Vietnam War, and now of the oil crisis, intensified the endemic inflation which distributes wealth in an erratic and often cruel way. Most important, Americans are unwilling to endure restraint.

A critic of Heilbroner, Christopher Freeman, has written an article in which he makes the perceptive comment that talk among the educated about the limits to growth may help turn undergraduates in selective colleges away from science and technology as evil in themselves, and thus worsen the very crisis which faces us. Freeman is not saying, and I am not, that there is any quick technological fix to our problems. Rather, what we need are leaders like President Carter, steeped in science and technology and at the same time capable of managing the traffic jams created by conflicting political and cultural expectations in a large and litigious society, who have supporters and followers able to assess realistically how we are to distribute and redistribute limited resources and to persuade people of the growing need for restraint, while still maintaining our productive capacity.

The career plans of college graduates over the last few years form a brain drain of gifted people into the law and even into medicine. These are seen as independent and autonomous professions—and the already arrived do not seek these professions primarily in order to make money. Rather, the professions are attractive because they appear to promise security in an occupationally threatening world, and because of the mistaken belief that they offer a road to personal independence; and because idealism and altruism can be served in community practice in medicine or through a law degree leading to various forms of poverty and public interest law and, indeed, to environmental litigation. However, it is worth pointing out that most lawyers and doctors are subject to the demands and expectations of clients and colleagues at least as imperative as would be the demands in working for IBM.

Managerial Framework

Let me clarify what may be a misunderstanding of my own moral perspective. This age cohort was born into a period of growing American affluence and into a situation of competition for a declining number of occupations considered "meaningful," since there are so many with excellent educations competing with each other. It is in precisely this framework that the human prospects for the current generation of young people are encompassed, once we assume the absence of nuclear war. We must prepare for what economist Kenneth Boulding terms the management of decline; and if it is the understanding and resolution of such hard choices which lies ahead for all of us, then it is important for today's college graduates to consider entering managerial occupations and not only the supposedly independent professional ones. Among these I include civil service to local, state, and federal governments, and entrepreneurial, high-technology corporations, many of them multinational, which will be essential for handling the still exigent problems of production that lie ahead.

If one should ask, "How are we to manage?" I would reply, "With strong leadership and with teamwork; certainly not by endless litigation." How else are we to resolve the tacit class conflicts between the already affluent who want clean air, water, and the survival of porpoises, as against the not yet affluent, some of whom would also like these amenities, but for whom immediate jobs and comforts newly attained are more important? How can we persuade the consumer movement that perhaps the greatest enemy of the consumer is American protectionism, which is destructive to countries like Japan and Italy which depend entirely or largely on exports? Our task is to relocate our inefficient textile workers, auto workers, steel workers, or whatever else we do inefficiently, in order to reduce inflation and to bind the world together in a less protectionist and tariff-minded fashion.

For some, it would not seem too late to embark on new, perhaps not yet even invented careers in the creative, nonlitigious, nonadversarial management of change. By change, I refer to this world we are entering of bottlenecks and scarcities, with their concomitant inflationary potentials, which will require not only new technologies for the whole society, but—more important—a new mentality and a temperate yet tough morality, a new way of handling conflicts of interest which does not strengthen the veto groups that now clog our courts, our governmental agencies at all levels, our Congress, and even our streets.

Two Levels

We must learn to live on two levels. On one, we look realistically at the world and take such steps as we can to insure that there will be human prospects and that we can find ways to mitigate the worst Malthusian disasters by foresight and restraint. But on the other level, we must also live from day to day with faith in humankind's potential, including the potential to recover from catastrophes. This is where we depend on the example of men like Anton Chekhov, who went to study the suffering prisoners on an island off Siberia, or, in a different vein, George Orwell—men who possessed the ability to live with awareness of evil, yet with the faith that while there is life, there are many human prospects not foreclosed. □

READINGS SUGGESTED BY THE AUTHOR:

Doty, Paul; Carnesale, Albert; and Nacht, Michael L. ''The Race to Control Nuclear Arms.'' *Foreign Affairs* 55 (October 1976): 119–32.

Kennan, George F. *American Diplomacy, 1900–1950*. Chicago: University of Chicago Press, 1951.

Mandelbaum, Michael. ''Nuclear Stability and Political Order: The First Nuclear Regime.'' In *Nuclear Weapons and World Politics*, edited by David Gompert. New York: McGraw-Hill, 1977.

Shulman, Marshall. ''On Learning to Live With Authoritarian Regimes.'' *Foreign Affairs* 55 (January 1977): 325–38.

Yergin, Daniel H. *Shattered Peace: Origins of the Cold War and the National Security State*. Boston: Houghton Mifflin, 1977.

CHILDREN'S RIGHTS

ELISE BOULDING
University of Colorado

The process of defining who is to be treated as a human being with publicly recognized rights has been a long, slow one. The 1780 French Declaration of the Rights of Man treated children as a residual category of persons without full human rights. The Universal Declaration of Human Rights, adopted unanimously by the UN General Assembly in 1948, neglected to mention the classificatory principle of age. Thus children are not protected by these declarations.

Children's Movement

Can a case be made that consideration of the rights of children should be included in the general process of consciousness raising about the human condition, which is what the human rights movement is all about, or do the particular biological characteristics of this population make it appropriate to handle it through protection, placing it under the care of middle-years adults? The slow but steady growth internationally of the children's rights movement since the 1960s suggests that a reconsideration of this issue is due.

The children's movement is really two movements: the children's movement proper, consisting largely of urban area young people between the ages of 8 and 14 and supporting adults; and the youth rights movement, including high school and college-age young people. That covers a large age span, but in terms of rights youth are classed with and treated as children. The middle-years apostles of rights for children and youth often write with the high passion characteristic of outraged friends of the oppressed, and can be easily ignored by rational people of goodwill.

Documents about youth published by the United Nations Educational, Scientific, and Cultural Organization (UNESCO) sometimes use the term "antiyouth racialism" to refer to the hostility toward youth which is expressed both in public policy and private utterance, particularly in Western countries. Further, Richard Farson's accusation that we have replaced ignorant domination of the child by sophisticated domination hovers uneasily over a careful reading of the Declaration of the Rights of the Child. So does Christiane Rochefort's poignant plea on behalf of children: that adults should stand on *their* side, not on the side of their exploiters.

Gerard Mendel proposes the development of class consciousness on the part of children, and the waging of a class struggle between children and adults, as a way of getting children on a more equal footing with their protectors. This is an unusual class war, for it is one which is to release the positive, creative force of childhood in all of us. Adults, finally seeing children in their own personhood, will recognize and respect the inward state of being a child as a valuable and permanent part of the human personality, not something to be outgrown or overcome, and rediscover the child in themselves. It is a war which everyone will win.

The theme of all human rights convenants, and the motif of all liberation movements, is participation in the shaping of one's own life and that of the society around one, and reasonable access to the resources that will make that participation possible. Either children are ignorant and incapable of significant social participation, and must be segregated from the adult world until they are 21 via the mechanism of the family so they will do as little damage as possible, or they are evolving participatory capabilities from early childhood and should be brought into gradual involvement in the public sphere—as well as in family duties and family decision making—as their interests and abilities determine.

If the latter is true, some substantial changes in the current Declaration of the Rights of the Child, and in associated concepts of the rights and responsibilities of children in families and communities, will be required, both in custom and in law. More than that, some substantial changes in our conception of world order processes will also be required. Since children represent well over 50 percent of the world's population at present, and are completely excluded from the reporting, evaluating, and policymaking processes of every society, an opening up of these processes to all young persons able to express interest and concern, of whatever age, would in the long run represent a revolution of uninmaginable proportions in every country in the world, to say nothing of in the United Nations itself.

The arena of public policy is both the first and the last place to look for significant social change toward a more just social order. If "UN Years" mean anything, they mean an opportunity to reexamine ends and means with regard to policy issues. The current UN Year of the Child offers policymakers a fresh place to start with issues of human welfare: at the intersection of child, adult, and local community relationships. A change in social attitudes toward children would affect every nook and cranny of society, and every person in it. Adult-child relationships offer a critical intervention point for breaking the vicious cycles of dominance behaviors that pervade public and international life. These patterns are laid down in the home with daily acts of inappropriate exercises of power, invisibly interwoven with the acts of human caring that sustain the institution of the family as a continuously viable setting for human growth.

We may be unnecessarily sabotaging our present and our children's future by being blind to the inconsistencies and irrationalities of adult-child interaction in family and community in this century. Mass media programs about the right to a happy and secure childhood, surrounded by loving adults, cannot substitute for the actual experience of frank and honest confrontation between generations when perceptions, needs, and interests differ, in a context of mutual acceptance of responsibility for each other. Neither can special feeding, health, and education programs undertaken *for* children substitute for joint community projects carried out by adults and children together, in which the capacities of the young to contribute to the welfare of all receives full recognition.

Chronological Age and Social Maturity

The legal ground for assigning legal minority or "nonage" to children and youth is that they are physically, emotionally, and socially immature beings who must be protected by adults until they reach full maturity and can cope on their own with society. In general, the term "children" is used for those under 12 or 14, and "youth" for those from the age of 14 or 15 to 21 or 25, the age sometimes going as high as 30. This means that society is protecting itself by legal means from having to incorporate young persons into full participation in society, for what may be as long as half or more of the lifetime of those persons.

Because age groups are designated in various ways in various societies, depending on custom, there is no standardized set of categories used in policy-making. Utilizing the United Nations demographic reporting categories, I will use the following categories, which correspond roughly with social usage and reporting on children in many countries: 0–9, children; 10–14, adolescents; 15–19, youth; and 20–24, young adults.

Some societies treat all persons under 25 as legal minors; more common usage is to treat all under 21 as legal minors, with 18 being established as the age of majority recently in a few countries. In many countries a young person of 20 is as much a minor as a newborn baby. A United Nations study of the young adult offender suggests that morphological, physiological, endocrinological, and other aspects of physical development are not complete in many individuals until some time after age 25, that psychological maturation peaks between 25 and 29 years of age, and that social maturation is reached still later. While this study may refer to some measurable body states, the significance of the concept of maturity in connection with adulthood and societal participation weakens when applied in this way.

The idea that there are built-in pathologies in modes of childrearing, particularly in the more "developed" and urban societies, which produce permanently immature and war-prone adults, is not a new one. It is gaining new ground through studies of patriarchy, militarization, and the conquest syndrome by researchers working in the interdisciplinary fields of peace studies, future studies, and human development. On the other hand, studies of cognitive, moral-emotional, and political maturity by developmental psychologists make it fairly clear that the basic intellecting capacities are present very young, and that complex moral and political reasoning can take place at least by the ages of 12 to 14—if not younger.

Maturity needs to be substantially redefined before it becomes a criterion for full participation in society. Even in our own century children from a very young age are required, as are women, to do heavy physical labor that in theory is not suited to their physical capacities. They serve and tend their own parents, and become parents themselves, all while still legally minors. They fight wars, mount relief operations, design international institutions—all between the ages of 12 and 21. It is only necessary for each of us to remember back to our own childhood, what we coped with, what insights we gained, to realize how much children endure, how much they have to give that adults never notice. What is maturity?

Children and Youth in the Labor Force

At present, adults professionally concerned with children are somewhat confused about what position they should take in regard to child labor. The anti-child labor movement in Europe and North America was very strong from the late nineteenth century through the early decades of this century. Factory conditions and working hours were terrible for young bodies and minds, and much of the spirit of protection that we see in the 1970s stems from the necessary drive to protect children from these abuses of an earlier stage of the Industrial Revolution.

Today's generation of children in the industrial West is told to run and play and study more. Ironically, these children feel trapped in the playroom and the schoolroom and would love to have their own job. Their despair is variously exhibited in high frequencies of suicide, of drug and alcohol use, and in rising school dropout rates. Both the younger 10–14 age group and the older 15–19 age group are affected.

Yet in most of the world children are at work by the age of 15. In fact, they are at work from the age of 5 in rural areas. Boys work in the fields; girls help with younger children, or help in household and field work also. They have always done so, from the time of the earliest hunting and gathering bands. With urbanization, working conditions become harder—whether we are talking about ancient or modern urbanization. In the 1970s, when children are supposed to be in school, there is little incentive to report child labor, and most children work unrecorded, whether for their own parents or as wage laborers.

The under-15s are the most vulnerable part of the work force, but young workers up to the age of 25 lack the protections that workers over 25 may receive, according to a UNESCO report. They bear the brunt of unemployment (sometimes as high as 50 percent unemployed) and they work much longer hours for lower wages. While many unions do not stipulate an age limit on union membership, the practice is to exclude them from work councils until they are 21 or even 23, thus effectively disenfranchising them. A few unions defend the interests of their younger workers, particularly in socialist countries, but most apparently do not. Frequently the stipulated age for union membership is higher than the minimum age for admission to employment. There is considerable evidence that working conditions can be very punitive for children and youth, beyond what they are for older workers. Since youth are also better educated than their parents, and taught to have higher aspirations, the alienation of children and youth from the concept of work as a positive social value is strong.

Since the need for children and youth (both the under-15s and the over-15s) to work appears to be overriding in societies at all stages of development, enfranchising them to negotiate their conditions of work side by side with older workers ought to be seriously considered. Antiwork laws do not provide a viable approach.

Military Service for Youth

If there has been confusion about policies regarding children and youth in the labor force, there has never been any confusion about policies regarding military service of young persons. Minors have always been put into armies, and there have been many teenage military heroes in history. One of the prophet Mohammed's greatest generals was turned down for military service by Mohammed at age 14, but accepted at age 15 as an officer. Alexander the Great was a veteran of many battles by the time he was 20. Henry V served as a general in his father's army, conducting the war against Wales at the age of 14.

Most countries have compulsory conscription. The length of service usually ranges from one to three years, and most nations do not have provision for alternative service for conscientious objectors. (Most countries do not conscript young women.) Young people who have been reared in dissenting pacifist sects—such as are found in all the major religious traditions of the world— frequently suffer severe persecution, imprisonment, and sometimes the death penalty when they are drafted into their country's military, because of the lack of provision for the pacifist conscience. Most young people become liable for military service by age 18. It is not difficult to see, therefore, that a substantial part of the burden of national defense in countries rests on the shoulders of youth under 21.

Bearers and Rearers of Children

We are so accustomed to the legal and social rhetoric about protecting minors that we forget that a great deal of the work of rearing and protecting the young is done by persons who are themselves still minors.

The significant aspect of teenage pregnancy is that it is not simply a phenomenon of less industrialized countries, but of the most industrialized countries, with the United States a leading producer of teenage mothers. The "prime time" for women to bear children is considered to be between the ages of 20 and 24. Earlier childbearing involves high risk to the mother, and considerably lowered chances of survival for the infant. Yet in many countries large numbers of teenage girls take these risks, at least in part because their minority status prevents them from gaining access to the preventive measures they could employ if they knew about them. In *no* society does minority status make sexual activity inaccessible, whatever the official norms might be.

The onset of fertility ranges from age 10 to the mid-teens. One of the tragedies for young girls is that while the majority of them live in countries where family planning services are available and abortion is legal under certain conditions, the 10–15-year-olds who are at risk of pregnancy almost never have access to these services. Even 15–19-year-olds are drastically underserviced in comparison to older women. Teenage women can and do seek illegal abortion, in ignorance of safer methods, and a recent study in Cali, Colombia estimated that complications from illegal abortions were the leading cause of death of women aged 15 to 35.

Since even the prime childbearing years of 20 to 24 are years in which young women are treated as youth, not attaining legal majority until age 21 in many cases, the great majority of young women enter childbearing with a legal handicap—as well as a physiological handicap if they bear before the age of 20. These young procreators represent a large proportion of the world's population. And since teenage childbearing lowers their life expectancy, in many countries young girls may already be into the last decade or two of their life when they begin childbearing.

The responsibilities of the teenage married woman who is also a mother may be light compared to the responsibilities of the teenage unmarried mother. Of the out-of-wedlock births in the United States, a majority of these young women keep their babies and have their lives programmed for them in terms of the double task of working to support the mother-child household, and of being sole parent to the child. Economic support from the father, even if paternal filiation is legally established, is rare. What percentage of these young mothers will eventually marry we do not know. We do know that they receive a disproportionately small share of publicly funded family planning services.

Married or unmarried, teenage mothers, like older mothers, bear the primary responsibility for parenting. Society neither expects parenting from fathers, of any age, nor gives them training for it. Among the most disadvantaged categories of minors, then, are the unwed adolescent and teenage mothers and their illegitimate offspring. While the Declaration of the Rights of the Child guarantees whatever rights there are to all children regardless of birth, in fact only twenty-two countries recognize one status for all children whatever their circumstances of birth. In all the rest both the unwed mothers and their illegitimate children carry lifelong handicaps.

The cards are stacked against the unwed mother and the illegitimate child in every conceivable way. Tribal customs which provide formulas for the legitimacy of any child born regardless of circumstances of birth are disappearing, to be replaced by inhumane "modern" laws. Given the rapid increase in percent of out-of-wedlock births in many countries, including the most industrialized, this creates a serious long-term problem as regards responsible citizenship in the world community. The full burden of this problem is placed squarely on the fragile shoulders of children and youth.

While the burdens placed on adolescent and teenage women are very heavy and may substantially shorten their life expectancy, it should also be emphasized that many of these unmarried child-mothers do in fact cope successfully with the burdens placed upon them. Many do make homes for their children; they do work to support them; they do provide nurture when they themselves have been without nurture. They give responsibility to their own children very early, just as they have had to take responsibility very early. Most researchers study the "problem" teenage mother households; few look at the ones who manage well. The strengths these young women exhibit under such great and prolonged stress are an indication of the resources available to society if they were allowed to participate in its shaping on more equal terms.

Nurture of Parents by Children and Youth

I have suggested the important role children must inevitably play as partner to the mother who is herself scarcely out of childhood in mother-headed households. The child as working partner in the family is as old as the phenomenon of the family itself. The child as nurturer of the younger and older members of the household is a role that is overlooked. On the one hand, uncounted numbers of children in the Third World (and the First) are cared for by siblings aged 8 to 12. On the other hand, children also provide nurturance to their own parents and grandparents. While this phenomenon is present in all societies, it is most apt to be recorded in the West, where there is an ample supply of professionally trained workers making observations on family behavior. This child-to-adult nurturance comes poignantly to view in discussions of abusing parents in the United States.

An exploratory project containing cross-cultural material on the extent to which teenagers counsel and give emotional support to parents in times of stress suggests that this is a very widespread phenomenon. Historically, children have acted as servants to their parents, at least in the West, and in preindustrial Europe this was well worked out in terms of exchange of children between households, so each set of parents trained their neighbors' children in household skills. A number of etiquette books were written for children in the Middle Ages and later advising them on their servant role, and it is clear that children had to be very resourceful, from the kinds of situations set out as teaching examples.

One of the least noticed times when children nurture parents is during a death in the family. The nurturing role of the child is even more important in family traumas of separation and divorce, traumas that are more difficult than bereavement because they take longer to play themselves out. Sometimes young people will drop out of high school or college to care for a parent who is overstressed during or after divorce. If one had to select for the most mature behavior in a stressed family, not infrequently one might select for the behavior of a child over that of the adults. A serious study of compassion and coping in preadolescent and adolescent children is long overdue. Indeed, the materials for a study of children as partners in the human enterprise are at hand. They have only not been utilized.

Shapers of the Future

The prolongation of childhood and dependency that the extension of school years has brought about in industrialized countries has led to a gradual forgetting on the part of adults about the roles that children and youth have always played in social change. Many of these have been tragic roles, such as in the Children's Crusades. Yet the quality of thought and action that has gone into the protest movements of children and youth should not be judged by their outcomes, for throughout history society has never welcomed the fresh insights of its youngest members.

Fourteen was not too young to be a peace activist in the 1960s. Furthermore, the teenage protest movement fought in Europe and the United States for the right to have high school chapters of the college-age radical social change organizations. Discovering that they had no freedom of association in their schools, they sometimes turned to civil liberties organizations for help in legal battles. They were and still are present in all the community-based movements to create alternative structures—free schools, people's clinics, refuges for children who do not wish to live with their parents. In the United States high school and college young people went to the 1971 White House Conference on Children and Youth and published minority reports on every topic, to counteract the protectionist line of the official proceedings. Little attention was paid to them, but they did it anyway.

University-age youth, many still legally minors, have their own international communications networks, and their activities for peace and social justice in the late sixties rocked the world community. While their actions are less dramatic now, their international institution building goes on. Young people in the student category have a long tradition, probably going back to the very inception of the institution of the academy of learning in the first millennium B.C., of social innovation. Sometimes it is highly visible; sometimes it is unnoticed and unsung.

Given the tendency for the traces of youthful activism to disappear from public consciousness, what happens to young activists when they reach their late twenties? An important recent comparative study of adults who were students at the centers of activism in the early 1960s in Japan and in the United States suggests that students who were active in the civil rights and peace movements of those times have continued to be activist and politically aware in the seventies. Further, according to UNESCO reports, although the character of youth activism has changed, the amount of activism is probably the same or somewhat increased.

Mainstream Youth Organizations

Many mainstream children's and youth organizations are run by professional adults on behalf of youth, but young people's developing skills of organization are beginning to make a new and more visible role for them in their own right. Young people have begun systematically to attend all UN conferences and make their own reports. Action lags far behind words, but at least the words are there.

The United Nations Commission on Human Rights has taken up the role of youth in the deliberations of UN bodies, and is considering the appointment by youth organizations in each country of a youth correspondent with the United Nations for issues related to human rights. Its commitment to the "development of youth projects with the purpose of identifying and examining situations where the human rights of young people are being seriously restricted or violated" is the opening wedge; it came about on the initiative of young people themselves. They are not asking for protection, but for participation.□

READINGS SUGGESTED BY THE AUTHOR:

Berg, Leila. "Moving towards Self-government." *In Children's Rights: Toward the Liberation of the Child*, edited by Julian Hall. New York: Praeger Publishers, 1971.

Farson, Richard. *Birthrights*. New York: Macmillan Publishing, 1974.

Foster, Henry H., Jr. *A "Bill of Rights" for Children*. Springfield, Ill.: Charles C. Thomas, 1974.

Hess, Robert D., and Torney, Judith V. *The Development of Political Attitudes in Children*. Chicago: Aldine Publishing, 1967.

Mendel, Gerard. "Introduction." In *Rights and Responsibilities of Youth*, compiled by the United Nations. Educational Studies and Documents, Number 6. Paris: UNESCO, 1972.

REPORTING RIGHTS CONFLICTS

JOHN CROTHERS POLLOCK and
JAMES LEE ROBINSON, JR.
Livingston College

How do human rights issues become stories printed in newspapers as part of their daily news agenda? What causes some rights issues to surface in every paper's news array, to join a "national agenda" of news stories, and how much regional and metropolitan variation emerges?

Human Rights Coverage

These questions are important, but their significance has been overlooked in most research on mass media performance. That research currently displays two major shortcomings. One is that studies adopt as a focus, as targets for explanation, the customary rhythms of formal political processes: political campaigns, routinized elections, and the press conferences of elected officials. A second deficiency of contemporary political communication research is its restricted, compartmentalized array of predictive factors, confining explanations to variations in reporter recruitment, work roles, socialization, and in news organizations, bypassing or belittling the social and political contexts in which newspapers are imbedded. These shortcomings can be addressed by examining press reporting on human rights issues.

Rights coverage can be studied in crisis conditions, moments when cherished values confront one another in sharp relief: when journalists, like other decision makers in public life, are compelled to make choices about the central issues of our time and to manifest those choices openly. A focus on what Sidney Kraus and David Davis call "critical events... which produce the most useful explanations and predictions of social change" may draw attention both away from reporting on elections as routinized choice points and toward crucial political tests (be they coups, strikes, civil disorders, key judicial decisions, or crucial referenda) confronting political systems.

Data Base

We will consider three "critical events" involving groups who claim their rights are endangered. The events include a prison uprising, a judicial decision, and a county referendum repealing an ordinance, specifically: the takeover of New York's State Correctional Facility at Attica on September 10, 1971, by prisoners, most of whom were black; the Supreme Court ruling on June 20, 1977, that states need not pay for abortions unless they are medically necessary; and the repeal by a two-to-one majority on June 7, 1977, of a Dade County, Florida ordinance protecting homosexuals from discrimination in employment, housing, and public accommodations. These three events raised issues of surpassing importance for blacks, women, and homosexuals.

The Attica rebellion dramatized complaints of prisoners generally and blacks in particular about prison conditions and the marginal life chances of blacks. The recent abortion decision raised compelling questions about individual liberty for both the unborn and women generally. The Dade County or "Miami" vote threw a national spotlight on claims made by homosexuals regarding discrimination in employment and housing. Each issue was a national event, inviting substantial coverage by papers throughout the country. Each issue also represented a "critical event" for each group, occasions for the exercise of newspaper choice and discretion in presenting news on human rights claims.

Like the adoption of new issue targets for communication research, a search for appropriate explanatory variables requires the mapping of new intellectual terrain. Many serious studies restrict predictive factors to reporter personalities, newsroom socialization and work roles, or the norms of professional journalism, overlooking the importance of community and even national news constraints. Significant questions about constraints can be tested by comparing newspaper coverage of the three selected events in five major cities in the United States. The papers are the *Boston Globe*, the *Chicago Tribune*, the *Los Angeles Times*, the *New York Times*, and the *Washington Post*.

What kinds of media agenda are produced for critical events involving disadvantaged groups? Are most newspapers consistent in their coverage, reflecting the emergence of a "national agenda" which contains the texture of discussion within predictable boundaries, or does reporting vary markedly from paper to paper, perhaps reflecting regional demographic or political variations? Those who expect production of a national agenda may look to Washington or New York for the source of that agenda, in the converging citadels of governmental, financial, and media influence. Those who expect regional agenda variations may look to the way media institutions are imbedded in local frameworks, rooted in diverse socioeconomic and community structures.

Regional variation apart, how much variation is evident within each paper in its treatment of black prisoners, women, and homosexuals? Is coverage of one group congruent with coverage of the others? Does there exist a "double standard" for reporting on rights claims? Or does each paper exhibit a rather consistent human rights perspective, no matter the group involved? Where variations in group coverage appear, do they reflect surrounding demographic influences?

Broad Coverage Patterns

Substantial differences among all five newspapers are revealed in their coverage of each group. Although a few similarities were apparent, as in the coverage given blacks in Attica by the *Washington Post* and the *Chicago Tribune*, and in the coverage of homosexuals by the *Washington Post* and the *Boston Globe*, each paper covered blacks, women, and homosexuals differently (see Table 1).

TABLE 1
Comparative Coverage of Human Rights Claims

Newspaper	Attica	Abortion	Miami Vote
Chicago Tribune	1	1	1
Boston Globe	2	2	4
Los Angeles Times	5	3	3
New York Times	4	4	2
Washington Post	3	5	5

Note: "1" is assigned to the newspaper with the least favorable or least legitimizing coverage of human rights claims; "5" is assigned to the newspaper with the most favorable or most legitimizing coverage of such claims.

Source: Data collected and tabulated by authors.

Two broad patterns merit attention. Three papers demonstrated a pattern of relatively strong legitimation or delegitimation of human rights claims generally. The *Chicago Tribune* consistently showed the poorest coverage, suggesting the possibility of a general delegitimizing orientation toward human rights claims, regardless of source. The *Washington Post*, aside from its negative coverage of Attica, tended to exhibit a general orientation toward human rights which is essentially legitimizing, in strong contrast to reporting found in the *Tribune*. The *Post*'s coverage of the abortion decision and the Miami vote were the most favorable for any of the papers sampled. The *New York Times* was similar to the *Post*, although it was the only newspaper other than the *Tribune* to reveal a negative, delegitimizing point of view in reporting on the Miami referendum on homosexuals.

The perspectives reflected by the *Los Angeles Times* and the *Chicago Tribune* together revealed a second pattern: consistent coverage of all three human rights issues. Regardless of the direction of the content, be it legitimizing or delegitimizing, coverage in both papers varied within an extremely small range.

What accounts for such divergent patterns from paper to paper, and for such consistency within papers in reporting on each group? Since newspaper variation is evident, the proposition that a national agenda might be set by national wire services or by prestige papers with their own news services, the *New York Times* and the *Washington Post*, can be discarded. Since so much consistency is apparent inside each paper in reporting on the claims of distinct groups, and since so many different reporters and editors were employed in writing such stories, variations in the background, socialization, and work roles of individual journalists are unlikely to explain a given newspaper's patterned reporting on reform efforts. Are there variations in the characteristics of cities which predict variations in what city newspapers print?

Metropolitan Area Factors

Two sets of metropolitan demographic indicators can be tested to determine their association with legitimizing or delegitimizing reporting. One set records the distribution or "presence" of blacks, women, and percent of the population below the "poverty level" (as established by the 1970 census) for each city. (Although the percentage of homosexuals for each city might be assumed proportional to population, no such assumption is made, since precise data are unavailable.)

The other set of indicators employed are education levels and religious membership (specifically in the Catholic Church) to suggest aggregate levels of "participation" or capacity for access to political, social, and communication institutions, of which newspapers are one category. The relative presence of blacks, women, and poor people is expected to have some impact on the propensity of newspapers to legitimize or delegitimize the claims of such groups. The presence of large numbers below the poverty level is assumed to have some bearing on the demand for access to public funds for abortions. It is provisionally assumed that the more blacks, women, and poor citizens present, the more likely a city's paper is to legitimize the rights claimed by such groups.

Similarly, the more participatory such groups generally, or the larger the membership of a group explicitly concerned with claims forwarded, the more newspapers can be expected to take group viewpoints seriously in their presentation of claims. The higher the education level of a group, the greater the capacity of that group for interest in and access to newspapers. In related fashion, the larger the membership of an organization (in this case a religious organization which opposes abortion and homosexuality because both interfere with procreation), the more likely a city paper is to legitimize that group's claims against those who support elective abortion and freedom from discrimination against homosexuals.

Media Coverage and Demographic Variables

Since each group's coverage is confined to only one critical event each, and since only three events are studied, precise conclusions must await a larger sample of both newspapers and occasions involving human rights claims. Three broad patterns are sufficiently clear to warrant attention and further testing.

First, with the exception of the abortion issue, indicators of demographic "participation" appear more powerful than simple indicators of "presence" in predicting legitimation of rights claims. Abortion aside, the strongest correlations between city characteristics and rights coverage are found among indicators of group participation (schooling for blacks and legitimizing coverage of prisoners of Attica, percent Catholic and legitimizing coverage of homosexuals in the context of the Miami vote). Even concerning the abortion issue, the correlation indicates that the higher the percent Catholic in a city's population, the more likely newspapers are to delegitimize efforts to retain public funds for elective abortions.

Demographic indicators of presence and participation differ in another way. Correlation of percent black, women, and poor with rights press coverage reveals substantial variation from issue to issue or group to group. Indicators of participation, by contrast, are far more consistent in predicting human rights coverage. Higher levels of schooling for blacks and women are almost always associated positively with legitimizing coverage of rights claims across all three issues. Higher percentages of Catholics are always associated negatively with claims on behalf of black prisoners, women, and homosexuals. Participation is both stronger and more consistent as a predictor of human rights coverage than is a population's presence or distribution.

A second general observation is that of all tested factors predicting coverage of rights claims, the strongest and most consistent is percent Catholic population in each city. Catholic membership is associated strongly with press coverage delegitimizing the claims of all three groups studied. This finding may reflect only the results of a small sample of coverage of three issues in five cities, each of which is a Catholic Archdiocese, a center of episcopal authority. But the strength and consistency of the associations compel attention to the religious factor in human rights discussions.

Finally, the press coverage most strongly associated with demographic variables is that related to homosexuals. Considering all correlations, in particular those associating social participation and rights coverage, relorting on the Miami vote appears to vary clearly with variations in schooling and Catholic membership. Explanations are only conjectural, but one possible reason for this finding is the recency of homosexuality as an issue in the public agenda presented by mass media. When an issue is relatively "new" in the sense that it has begun to appear in print only recently, newspaper treatment may be highly sensitive to its local and regional demography or reading "constituency."

It can be further observed that correlations involving another recent public issue, the abortion controversy, are generally stronger than those referring to much older public claims regarding prisoner (and black) rights. Demographic variations appear relatively important in the coverage of issues surfacing recently.

Contextual Responses

Nationwide reporting on the rights claims of black prisoners, women, and homosexuals reveals provocative patterns. No "national agenda" for human rights reporting is evident; each newspaper treats these issues differently. At the same time, several major papers individually exhibit relatively consistent, general "human rights" perspectives which are maintained in considering the claims of diverse groups. In our sample the *Chicago Tribune* delegitimizes such claims more than other papers. At the other extreme, the *Washington Post* legitimizes the claims of two of these three groups more than other papers.

An initial test of demographic factors suggests three general patterns: the relative importance of indicators of "social participation" (Catholic membership and education) compared with group "presence" or distribution; the extremely strong association between Catholic membership and reporting delegitimizing rights claims; and the significance of an issue's recent "emergence" in predicting a paper's sensitivity to demographic variations. These conclusions are consistent with a broad perspective in which it is expected that newspapers, like other public institutions, are responsive to surrounding social and political contexts.

This contextual anchoring has been markedly overlooked in a substantial amount of mass communication research. Jeremy Tunstall has written extensively about the socialization and recruitment of reporters. Gaye Tuchman has studied newsroom interaction and expectations, Leon Sigal the professional and behavioral norms and "routines" of journalism, while Edward J. Epstein deals with profit making as an organizational imperative in the presentation of television news. Such studies are insightful, but their focus implies a locus of explanation rooted at the level of individual journalists, their background and socialization, or of newsrooms and news agencies. Relatively little attention is paid to community or "constituency" variation.

Political Focus

This article suggests the centrality of a focus on political and human rights. Other questions shrink in importance when compared with issues about the survival or resurrection of concern for fundamental human liberties. A concern with human rights and the way they are respected in the mass media may complement an interest in more familiar routines of politics: the committees, the licensing, even the less frequent but nevertheless regular periodicity of campaigns and elections.

These activities are useful *contexts* in which to study political communication, but they furnish few clues about the type of research to be performed. That research, whatever its locus, might appropriate as its central pivot questions about human rights: their legitimacy, violation, and protection. In this way social scientists can join policymakers in providing a concrete political focus to examine media performance when covering fundamental issues affecting lives.

READINGS SUGGESTED BY THE AUTHORS:

Ball-Rokeach, Sandra J., and DeFleur, Melvin L. "A Dependency Model of
    Mass-Media Effects." *Communication Research* 3 (January 1976): 3–21.
Goldenberg, Edie N. *Making the Papers: The Access of Resource-Poor Groups to the
    Metropolitan Press.* Lexington, Mass.: D.C. Heath, Lexington Books, 1975.
Kraus, Sidney, and Davis, David. "Critical Event Analysis." In *Political
    Communication: Issues and Strategies for Research*, edited by Steven Chaffee.
    Beverly Hills, Calif.: Sage Publications, 1975.
Sigal, Leon R. *Reporters and Officials.* Lexington, Mass.: D.C. Heath, Lexington
    Books, 1973.
Tichenor, Phillip J.; Roden-Kirchen, Jane M.; Olien, Clarice N.; and Donohue, George
    A. "Community Issues, Conflict, and Public Affairs Knowledge." In *New
    Models for Mass Communication Research*, edited by Peter Clarke. Beverly
    Hills, Calif.: Sage Publications, 1973.

TERROR

CHALMERS JOHNSON
University of California at Berkeley

The summer 1976 hijacking of an Air France plane by Palestinian terrorists and the spectacular rescue at Entebbe of some one hundred hostages by Israeli commandos once again focused world attention on the problem of terrorism. Four years earlier it was the Munich Olympics, when eleven Israeli athletes were killed; and in May 1972 it was the attack on Lod Airport, resulting in the deaths of twenty-six innocent bystanders and two of the terrorists.

Each time an event of such magnitude occurs, people stop and ask themselves what can be done to prevent it. Yitzhak Rabin gave his own answer to this question when he said of the Entebbe rescue operation, "It is Israel's contribution to the fight against terrorism, a fight that has not yet ended." Like the United States, Israel has so far maintained a hard-and-fast policy of refusing to negotiate with terrorists; but both countries have been criticized abroad and domestically for this position. Other countries—West Germany, Britain, and Japan, to name only a few—have given in to terrorist demands, with the frequent result that more terrorist acts followed.

State Department Conference

In March 1976 the U.S. State Department held a two-day conference on terrorism attended by some two hundred specialists on the subject (including academics, police and army officers, and diplomats) from both the United States and foreign countries. Among the issues discussed were the nature of terrorism, its causes, and how it could be controlled. That no consensus emerged on any of these issues, even among people who were in general agreement that terrorism ought to be stopped, indicates how complex the subject is.

Take the most basic question of defining terrorism. One speaker defined terrorism as political, goal-oriented action, involving the use or threat of extraordinary violence performed for psychological rather than material effect, and the victims of which are symbolic rather than instrumental. This seems like a perfectly straightforward definition, but already it raises certain questions. Does it exclude assassinations of political leaders which are not performed for psychological effect, but to eliminate these leaders and bring about political change? Does an attempt to outlaw terrorism, in short, also outlaw tyrannicide? Or, to put it another way, is one person's terrorist another's freedom fighter?

In view of the terrorist activities currently being directed against Jews and Israelis, it is worth recalling that the Jews themselves employed terrorism to devastating effect against the British in Palestine. The activities of the Irgun Svai Leumi and the Stern Gang included the murder of Lord Moyne on November 6, 1944; the blowing up of the King David Hotel in Jerusalem on July 22, 1946; the hanging of two British army sergeants whose bodies were found at the end of July 1947; and the murder of Count Bernadotte on September 17, 1948. In fact, it was this terrorist campaign that contributed to the British decision to give up the Palestine Mandate.

Typology of Terrorism

To say that one person's terrorist might be another's freedom fighter is to recognize, at a bare minimum, that not all terrorist organizations are alike and that we need a typology of terrorism. Typologies are based upon observation of differences and upon the attempt to discover the principles causing the differentiation. Thus one of the simplest, observation-based typologies of terrorist movements distinguishes four species in the genus terrorism: ethnic (including religious, linguistic, regional, or other particularistic movements), nationalistic (irredentist or anticolonial), ideological (including anarchist, radical leftist, orthodox communist, extreme rightist, and others), and pathological (including groups that attack public targets for apparently private, biographical reasons—for example, the Manson gang).

What are the principles that inform this typology? First, movements differ according to their ''legitimacy potential,'' meaning that a terrorist organization may be formed of a minority that is never likely to attract significant popular support, or a minority that has the potential of becoming a mass movement. Second, terrorist organizations differ by their principal audiences and by the reactions they aim to create through terrorist deeds. It may be true that the victims of terrorism are only symbolic, but it is necessary to ask, ''symbolic of what?'' An elite? A race? A government? A class?

Do terrorist groups ever have a ''legitimacy potential''? The answer seems to vary according to the degree to which a terrorist group is committed or drawn exclusively to the tactic of terrorism, and according to the degree to which a terrorist group is only part of or an offshoot of a larger movement of authentic revolution. Those groups explicitly committed to acts of terrorism are likely to degenerate into criminal gangs, as has happened often in the past. But terrorist organizations may be part of a wider politicomilitary scheme of revolution, such as in Algeria, Indochina, Latin America, and elsewhere. In these cases the resort to terrorism is not necessarily evidence of a low legitimacy potential. Terrorism may be pursued in the hope of producing a damaging overreaction by the defending side or as a means of purging and hardening the ideologically defined "people" in preparation for revolutionary war.

Increasing Trend

Regardless of whether one thinks that terrorism is sometimes justified, there is no question that it has greatly increased in the last few years. One study which has counted the international terrorist incidents that occurred between January 1, 1968 and December 31, 1975 found that there were 913 such incidents, including 123 kidnappings, 31 barricade and hostage episodes, 375 uses of explosive devices, 95 armed assaults or ambushes, 137 hijackings of aircraft or other means of transportation, 59 incendiary attacks or cases of arson, 48 assassinations, and 45 cases of other forms of violence. In these incidents a total of 800 people were killed and 1,700 were injured.

More alarming, the study found that a rapid rise in the number of terrorist incidents has been taking place. Between 1965 and late 1968 the number of cases remained below 50 a year. Then, in 1969–70, the rate jumped to well over 100 a year, fell back to around 75 during 1971, and ascended steeply to over 200 during 1973. It then declined slightly and remained at around 175 incidents per year through the end of 1975.

Direct and Permissive Causes

What has caused this increase? The causes of terrorism are generally divided into two broad classes—direct and permissive causes. Direct causes refer to grievances or frustrations, such as neocolonialism, ethnic dependence, or other alleged victimizations of groups of people, that may lead activists to resort to political violence. Permissive causes are those factors that make terrorism possible, even easy, and that therefore recommend it as a tactic for extremists. This distinction should not be made too rigidly, however, since lack of alternatives to terrorism can be understood as either a direct or an enabling cause. Similarly, the availability of publicity through news media should be viewed as a permissive cause in most cases; but publicity may also lead to a contagion or imitation effect, which can in turn become a direct cause of subsequent acts of terrorism. Thus the direct and permissive causes may differ between a single terrorist act and a cycle or epidemic of terrorism.

The direct cause most frequently cited in connection with terrorism is socioeconomic deprivation. If people were not so poor or so politically oppressed, the argument goes, they would not resort to terrorism. Unfortunately, in concrete cases of terrorism it is often very hard to separate the socioeconomic causes from much more psychological or pathological factors. In the Lod Airport massacre, for example, the terrorists were Japanese, recruited and trained through agents in North Korea, supported by funds from West Germany, given final training in Syria and Lebanon, armed in Italy, and sent to a destination unknown to them in advance by the Popular Front for the Liberation of Palestine. The sole surviving terrorist has testified that he became involved primarily because of the influence of his elder brother, and he has shown signs of severe mental disorientation in captivity. In this case the "direct" causes of the incident seem unlikely to have been removed even if the Arab-Israeli conflict were somehow resolved.

Some people argue that the direct causes of terrorism are to be found in the major social movements of the postwar era, particularly decolonization, and that a decline in terrorism can be expected because decolonization is virtually complete. Others have speculated that terrorism may be directly related to cyclical fluctuations in the overall economic climate—economic upturns allegedly promote terrorism by heightening expectations, while economic downturns may dampen revolutionary ardor through the numbing effects of general adversity—or that extracyclical worldwide economic strains, such as the quadrupling of oil prices, may have something to do with the rise in terrorism by overtaxing the capabilities of local regimes to govern effectively. The increasing bureaucratization of the world has also been cited as a direct cause: terrorism is thought to relate to bureaucracy as tyrannicide does to tyranny.

Despite such conjectures about direct causes, there is general agreement among students of the subject that the direct causes of terrorism have remained relatively constant in recent times and that the rise in international terrorist incidents is due almost entirely to changes in the permissive causes. These permissive causes have been given many names, such as "resentment, means, publicity, and low risk" or "feasibility, efficacy, and popularity." I have chosen to summarize them as the "three T's": targets, technology, and toleration. International terrorism has been on the increase during the past eight years because of the availability of new targets, new technology, and new toleration.

New Targets

By new targets I mean vulnerabilities or bottlenecks in advanced, open, industrial societies that make suitable targets for terrorist attack. These include large aircraft, supertankers, international power grids and pipelines, transportation hubs, commercial and communications centers, motorcades, off-shore oil rigs, liquified natural gas facilities, nuclear power plants, and computerized information and management systems.

The very existence of a complex and interdependent modern world seems to have contributed to the advance of terrorism by offering the terrorist a plethora of vulnerable targets. Some people despair over any society's ability to defend such targets, but the analytical solution to this problem would be to build sufficient redundancy into modern systems so as to avoid vulnerable bottlenecks. For example, transportation systems should seek a mix of automobiles, public transit, waterborne, and short- and long-range air transport, in order to avoid offering critical vulnerabilities, just as communications should be diversified among ground lines, microwave, satellite, and other technologies.

New Technology

New technology includes two separate aspects: new weapons and new means whereby the terrorist can capture global attention. In addition to the traditional arsenal of time bombs, machine guns, and plastic explosives, modern technology has contributed the miniaturized letter bomb; the man-portable guided missile (such as the Soviet SA-7 heat-seeking rocket); chemical, biological, and radiological agents; and the potentiality of using nuclear weapons. Two SA-7's were captured in the hands of Arab terrorists at the end of a runway in Rome in 1973, and radioactive iodine was employed in a terrorist incident in Austria in 1974.

Equal to or greater in importance than new weaponry in the growth of terrorism is the global expansion of mass media of communications. Since public attention to his cause is usually one of the terrorist's key objectives, advances in communications have been critically valuable to him. Media contribute to publicity for a particular terrorist cause, the contagious triggering of other terrorists' decisions to act, the training of terrorists through a media-fed pool of experience and inspiration, and international linkages among terrorist organizations.

New Toleration

The third of the permissive causes is a new toleration for terrorism. This includes direct and indirect support of terrorist organizations by nations, toleration of terrorism by law-abiding nations because of fears of retaliation, the failure to elicit international cooperation in carrying out countermeasures, and the increased legitimization of "revolutionary" activities. Among the so-called subversive centers for the training and support of terrorists, by far the most important are the Soviet Union and related Eastern European regimes; but also listed and described by various authorities are Libya, Cuba, China, North Korea, Algeria, the Popular Democratic Republic of Yemen, Tanzania, the Republic of the Congo (Brazzaville), Uganda, Zaire, Egypt, Syria, Iraq, Lebanon, and, recently retired from the business (but apparently not from state terrorism), Chile. Such centers supply terrorists with funds, arms, training, documentation, and operational support.

In a somewhat different category is the "humanitarian" aid supplied to revolutionaries in Mozambique, Guinea-Bissau, and Angola by Sweden, Denmark, Holland, Norway, Finland, and the World Council of Churches. Although not consisting of guns, this assistance has contributed to the climate of toleration of terrorist acts. In still another category are France and Switzerland, which have become involuntary hosts to all manner of foreign dissident groups because of their heritage of strong rights of political asylum and of protection of democratic freedoms. And in still a third category are those nations (for example, Japan) that are inhibited by political or commercial interests from offending governments that support or condone terrorism. They may also be concerned that if they convict and imprison terrorists, they will only attract more terrorists to their territories seeking, through further violence, to free their comrades.

For all of these reasons international efforts to stop terrorism have been very weak, and this toleration of terrorism has contributed to its spread. One recent study indicates that since 1968 an international terrorist involved in a kidnapping has an 80 percent chance of escaping death or capture, a close to even chance that all or some of his ransom demands will be granted, and the virtual certainty that he will receive worldwide publicity. For all crimes of terrorism the average sentence for the small proportion of terrorists caught and tried is less than eighteen months.

Antiterrorist Governments

In addition to the direct causes and the "three T's," one final factor that appears to be promoting the spread of international terrorism should be mentioned. This is the proliferation of antiterrorist authoritarian governments. Rigid and effective authoritarian rule may be fostering international terrorism by closing the main target systems to dissidents and forcing them to operate abroad.

It has been suggested that the situation today among various Latin American revolutionaries (particularly those from Brazil, Chile, Uruguay, and post-Peronist Argentina) may be somewhat parallel to that of Palestinian terrorists in the late 1960s. Being frustrated in their attempts to pressure Israel directly, the Palestinians sought to dramatize their cause by attacking more accessible societies. Similarly, Latin American revolutionaries, frozen out of their own societies, may be preparing to enter the international terrorist arena with attacks in North America.

The spread of authoritarian governments is a curious instance of the chicken-or-egg question, since it can be seen as both a cause of terrorism (internationally) and a consequence of terrorism (domestically). Several regimes faced with terrorist campaigns have managed to overcome them, but they have also lost their democratic institutions in the process. The best example is probably Uruguay, which between 1968 and 1971 was ravaged by the Tupamaros. Between April and August 1972, however, President Juan-Maria

Bordaberry broke the movement by proclaiming a "state of internal war" and giving the army and police complete freedom in their choice of methods. The Tupamaros are now gone, but democracy has not returned. Similar governmental strategies seem to be currently under way in Argentina and Chile.

Reducing Terrorism

What, then, can we reasonably expect to do about terrorism? On the international level, few positive steps have been taken to diminish terrorist activity. Legal specialists are fond of recommending new international law conventions on terrorism, but there seems to be some confusion about the status of the international law that already exists. In 1970 the United Nations General Assembly enacted its Declaration of Principles of International Law Concerning Friendly Relations and Cooperation Among States in Accordance with the Charter of the United Nations. This document states, on the one hand, that "every state has the duty to refrain from organizing, instigating, or participating in acts of civil strife or terrorist acts in another state or acquiescing in organized activities within its territory directed toward the commission of such acts," while, on the other hand, it obligates states to assist peoples struggling for the realization of their "right to self-determination and freedom and independence."

In light of these ambiguities and the poor track record of nations in ratifying or conforming to international conventions, new UN actions are not likely to resolve the freedom fighter versus terrorist dispute. Additionally, there are already on the books the 1963 Tokyo Convention on Offenses and Certain Other Acts Committed on Board Aircraft, the 1970 Hague Convention for the Suppression of the Unlawful Seizure of Aircraft, the 1973 Montreal Convention for the Suppression of Unlawful Acts Against the Safety of Civil Aviation, the 1973 UN Convention on the Prevention and Punishment of Crimes Against Diplomats (only nine ratifications to date and not in force), and the 1971 OAS Convention to Prevent and Punish Acts of Terrorism Taking the Form of Crimes Against Persons and Related Extortion that are of International Significance.

Until it was recently renounced by Cuba, the most useful international agreement to reduce terrorism was the 1973 U.S.-Cuba memorandum of understanding concerning hijackers of aircraft and vessels. Another achievement was the virtual elimination of aircraft hijacking in the United States through the use of physical inspection of all passengers and their hand baggage. The expense of this program argues against its extention to all exposed systems, but it may become necessary to consider some comparable measures such as the X-raying of mail at vital points. It is sometimes suggested that the automatic use of capital punishment would be effective against terrorists, but this has been hotly debated. Psychiatrists note, for example, that many would-be airplane hijackers have suicidal personalities and that a bloody shoot-out in which a hijacker is killed usually triggers several imitative hijacking attempts. If an automatic death penalty were instituted, they argue, more rather than few hijackings might result.

There has also been much debate over the policy, in force in the United States, of publicly declaring in advance that a government will not negotiate with terrorists under any circumstances versus the policy of reserving one's options and tailoring responses to particular cases. Those who have had direct experience in dealing with terrorists advocate the policy of no negotiations, arguing that it has prevented the spread of terrorism and worked as a deterrent. But many specialists doubt this, and some have suggested that the seizure of a Soviet embassy in a Western capital would be a hard test of the policy.

There is also the dilemma of multinational corporations faced with kidnappings of their executives: if they adopt a policy of no concessions they soon find themselves unable to retain their personnel or send them abroad. Many corporations have wanted to obtain tax credits for the ransom payments they have been obliged to make, and some have suggested that a form of "terrorism insurance" be made available. Most specialists take a dim view of both of these suggestions, since it is likely that they would only increase the instances of terrorism for ransom.

Since we lack an effective international convention against terrorism, there continues to be a great need for an enhanced intelligence capability against terrorists and for timely exchanges of intelligence information among cooperating security forces. It was through intelligence that the terrorists armed with SA-7's were apprehended at the edge of the airport in Rome before they could destroy their intended El Al Airlines target. The Israeli commando raid on Entebbe Airport was obviously also made possible through superb intelligence. Unfortunately, in the United States the need for counterterrorist intelligence comes precisely at a time when political circles are making efforts to prevent or restrict the collecting of such information.

Threat to Civil Liberties

The main issue today is whether terrorism can be suppressed. Some hold that it cannot be eliminated and warn against the dangers of overreaction. They feel that domestic criminal processes are adequate to deal with the problem, and that new countermeasures are not indicated. Others vehemently disagree and cite the costs of not dealing with terrorism or of naively believing that terrorism cannot thrive in an open society with few structurally generated grievances. Commentators from Great Britain, for example, argue that with respect to Ireland, Britain has in effect been experimenting with a policy of tolerating terrorism and that the results have been disastrous. In short, the costs of believing that "the cure could be worse than the disease" could be, on the one hand, a terrorist victory and the probable establishment of a totalitarian regime, or, on the other hand, a military-authoritarian reaction leading to the more or less permanent suspension of civil liberties.

For those, including myself, who feel that terrorism can and must be suppressed, the problem is less the defeat of terrorism than the avoidance of measures that may foreclose the rights and liberties characteristic of open, pluralistic societies. Terrorism can be suppressed through "special powers," but these inevitably entail a temporary curtailment or suspension of certain liberties. For example, censorship and detention without trial may be necessary. In order to insure that these measures do not lead to authoritarianism, special powers must be voted by parliaments—on the analogy of special powers enacted "for the duration" of a war against an external enemy.

The real problem of the suppression of terrorism is that elected assemblies *must* act in order to retain their sovereignty, and far too often they have delayed doing so until it was too late. "Paradoxically, then," as the distinguished English analyst Brian Crozier has put it, "the proclamation of a 'state of emergency,' martial law, or a 'state of internal war,' by the elected assembly, retaining its own sovereignty and therefore its right to revert to normal procedures, may be the only way of avoiding the military-authoritarian takeover. Sovereign assemblies that fail to act in good time clearly do so at their peril, if recent history is any guide." □

READINGS SUGGESTED BY THE AUTHOR:

Hutchinson, Martha C. "The Concept of Revolutionary Terrorism." *Journal of Conflict Resolution* 16 (September 1972): 383–96.

National Advisory Committee on Criminal Justice Standards and Goals. *Report of the Task Force on Disorders and Terrorism*. Washington, D.C.: Law Enforcement Assistance Administration, 1976.

Paust, Jordan J. "A Survey of Possible Legal Responses to International Terrorism: Prevention, Punishment, and Cooperative Action." *Georgia Journal of International and Comparative Law* 5 (1975): 431–69.

U.S. Central Intelligence Agency. *International and Transnational Terrorism: Diagnosis and Prognosis*. Washington, D.C.: Library of Congress, April 1976.

Wilkinson, Paul. *Political Terrorism*. London: Macmillan, 1974.

SURVIVAL

MARCUS G. RASKIN
Institute for Policy Studies / Transnational

P ractical concern with human rights is the life instinct of civilization. Without a shared consciousness and means for their application, there is little chance that humanity and civilization will be able to survive the next fifty years without horrifying and devastating tragedies. It goes without saying that any progress which human civilization might make is utterly tied to the meaning that human rights is given in the daily practice of nations and peoples.

Some will say that there is nothing "new" in the collective horror of this century, where reason is detached from personal feeling and subjective understanding. But they would be wrong. Our sophisticated, calculative intelligence is translated into military technologies of violence in being, like missiles, thermonuclear weapons, smart bombs, prisons, torture chambers.

Others will say that there is nothing new in huge bureaucratic structures where people are reduced to roles of processor and processed, joined together in a Kafkaesque embrace waiting for each to exchange roles. But there is a difference between this and other times. By virtue of what technology allows, there do not have to be limits to behavior. And that is what has happened.

Defining Human Rights

There is another side. Silently people cry out "enough," in a world gone morally and legally mad, where few either speak for humankind or with a human face. But a half-awakened consciousness of people is slowly becoming aware of a membrane which holds civilization together. It is this membrane, human rights, which is our task to nurture and strengthen, bringing intellectual and political sustenance to those rights. This task is not easy because the very nature and definition of human rights is ambiguous.

In our time the concept of human rights emerged from World War II, where cruelty and abomination had reached stunning proportions. It emerged from a period in which human beings had been the "objects" of Great Powers with virtually no standing in international law, and where the individual person's life was open to intrusion and destruction by states or the games which statesmen play with each other. The League of Nations took no notice of the internal affairs of states no matter how brutal the result, and leaders were not thought to be responsible for their actions in international law. It took World War II to recognize that there is a link between respect for freedom within the state and the maintenance of peace between states. The UN Charter reflects this point of view and recognizes human rights in the preamble.

It is important to remember the historical, moral, legal, and even psychological relationship between the Charter of Nuremberg (which attempted to develop a definition of personal responsibility), the United Nations Charter, and the later Human Rights Declaration. The Charter of Nuremberg, which was narrowly interpreted by judges, had sweeping and high purposes. The articles themselves either overlap or deal with those questions which *in practice* are human rights questions, questions which determine whether a state is something other than the means to organize people into submission or violence. The tribunal sought individual responsibility in three areas: crimes against peace, war crimes, and crimes against humanity.

As Richard Wasserstrom has pointed out, the principle of vicarious liability, which would hold members of a conspiracy responsible regardless of whether they had committed a particular act, was also introduced. Thousands of people were brought to justice under this charter and a similar one in Japan. Nuremberg is a stubborn fact of international affairs; it is a precedent that will not go away. Indeed, it is critical to our present understanding of international politics and law.

Promoting Human Rights

Simultaneous to the emergence of the Cold War and the breakup of old empires, the need appeared to forge some other, more positive direction which would limit the destruction of man's institutions upon people themselves. Nuremberg and the UN Charter were such imperfect instruments. The objective of the United Nations as laid out in the charter did not mean that there was a list of formal obligations in human rights which were a condition precedent to membership in the United Nations. Nevertheless, even without an explicit provision dealing with formal obligations, it would be absurd to think that the members of the United Nations did not formally accept the principles of respect for human rights. But respect, of course, is not the same as legal commitment.

The question of how to promote human rights in practice foundered on the rock of political sovereignty, legal imprecision, and bureaucratic fear and the Cold War. With the passage of the Universal Declaration of Human Rights in 1948, the world's people learned how limited—if any existed at all—were the obligations of the states to either apply or sign and implement by treaty the declaration's provisions. Mrs. Roosevelt, as chairwoman of the Commission on Human Rights, stated prior to its passage that the declaration was not a treaty or agreement; yet the declaration carried moral weight with the mass of people.

The declaration made clear that human rights were more than a "luxury." The declaration was more than the culmination of the ideologies which centered around natural law or those which centered around the cartoon of the inevitability of progress, a conception which had so gripped the pre-World War I socialist and liberal thinkers. The miracle of that document was that people with opposed ideologies had agreed on a basic list of rights although they could not state *why* they favored those rights as basic, how the definition of those rights would operate in practice, or a common philosophical understanding of the world.

American Ambiguity

Disagreement about first principles made it very difficult to develop a series of practices which would cause the enforcement of the Universal Declaration. While the document was predicated on many American notions, such as those laid out in the American Declaration of the Rights and Duties of Man (Bogota Conference of American States, 1948) and the thoughts of President Roosevelt's New Deal, and while diligent efforts caused the declaration to be quickly adopted, the United States did not accede to the document as a legally binding one, claiming that it had no such force. The document was seen by nations as an exercise in moral *oughtness*. The Soviets, however, appeared to want to give the declaration greater legal weight, as did the French and Belgians.

Early on the United States faced a hornet's nest with the passage of the declaration; and by the time that Eisenhower and Dulles came to power in 1953, the stage was set for the United States to withdraw any sort of support for effective human rights treaties. The reason the United States took this position during the time of Eisenhower is a complex one. In part, it was related to the conservatives in Congress and the Republican party who feared that the United Nations, and other nations as well, would upset the internal social system of the United States with "socialistic" ideas. There had been evidence that the U.S. courts were referring to the UN Charter in various of their decisions.

There was also a more complicated foreign policy reason. Dulles had enunciated the doctrine of liberation for Eastern Europe in the 1950–54 period. Except for covert operations, this reflected Cold War rhetoric more than the actualities of military intervention. Dulles feared that human rights covenants and declarations could be used by those to his political right or liberal interventionists to insist that the United States use such treaties as legalistic instruments for military action in Eastern Europe, a direction which he had no interest in implementing by force—as shown in the 1956 event of the Hungarian Revolution.

Helsinki Accords

But a generation is a long time in the history of international affairs. Friends become enemies, disputes which are thought of as settled flare up, ideas and goals thought of as too difficult to achieve become important questions to discuss and negotiate. The Helsinki Conference on Security and Cooperation in Europe set the diplomatic terms of reference for future U.S. diplomatic policy regarding Eastern Europe and human rights in Europe. Politically it is seen as a fine line between disengagement and liberation and means to reintegrate Europe. On the Western side, what could not be done by the spice of "rollback" was to be accomplished by the sugar of détente.

For our purposes, however, the human rights aspects to the Helsinki Accords are critical. The same secretary of state who objected to the American ambassador giving "political science lessons" to the Chilean junta when he complained about Chilean torture, accepted the human rights sections of the Helsinki Accords. The language of this document is similar in purpose and intent to the Universal Declaration, tracking the ideas of that document.

The more specific meaning of this section of the accords has been interpreted to apply to increased human contacts between Warsaw and NATO bloc nations. But the Helsinki Accords do nothing to point up the criminal nature of the arms race, calling instead for "confidence-building measures" such as "prior notification of major military maneuvers, exchange of observers" which "by their nature constitute steps towards the ultimate achievement of general and complete disarmament under strict and effective international control, and which should result in strengthening peace and security throughout the world."

What can we conclude from this litany of new good intentions? Moral pretension plays an important role in the statements, if not in the actions, of states; and while such pronouncements may be pronounced as cynical, it is also true that governmental energy is often spent explaining how the action of the particular state is in the path of moral righteousness and decency. This is understandable since most statesmen recognize, consciously or unconsciously, that both a state and the law which it uses and lives under require a moral basis if either the particular law or the state is to have any lasting significance—especially during a period of great transformation and turbulence. Without a moral basis which can be recognized as such by those who are not part of that particular system of beliefs, one may be sure that such laws or that state will become casualties of social transformation and world opinion. We see this phenomenon operating in southern Africa, and we saw it as well in the thirty-five year struggle against outside domination waged by the Vietnamese people.

Human Rights and the Arms Race

Certain rights have stood the test of time and the test of modern revolution as the basis upon which the people's freedom, and their own hopes, are to be staked. These freedoms can be added to and deepened in meaning as people discover more clearly the needs necessary to help them in their active subject role in history. The human rights of any particular period are rights necessary for people to exist and thrive in that particular historical period. But rights also are cumulative. Free speech or assembly is no less important because economic security is guaranteed in a society. Nor is it the case that the rights of economic security cease to exist because there is free speech and assembly. Rights in this sense are additive, not contradictory.

These rights, critical as they are and central to our present dilemma, are merely the beginning of understanding the problem of human rights as we should now come to consider it. In this sense we are confronted with an irony. The declaration, which should have been translated from "oughtness" to legally binding treaties a generation ago, is not adequate to face the present turbulent world because of the generally limited or ambiguous definition of human rights which is seen as applying to individuals, but not to individuals as part of a collective or class that can seek relief *prior* to an action of states. Thus it would seem that genocide has to be completed before there is acknowledgment that genocide has occurred.

The United States is in an even more troubling situation conceptually and morally. The Genocide Treaty has yet to be ratified by the U.S. Senate. Nor is the arms race and arms preparation recognized as part of the way that human rights are violated, or a crime nationally or internationally committed. Instead, nations see arming only as "defense."

The question of human rights must be linked to issues concerning the arms race and war. The direct nexus between the idea of human rights and the existing law of war was not envisaged until World War II was over. The nexus that the charter framers saw between the criminality of state aggression by armed forces and the denial of human worth within the frontiers of such states, and then repeated and increased in the areas that military adventures subjected to their occupation, rammed home in a way that mankind was not likely to forget the connection between aggressive war, the way it is waged, and the total disregard of the individual. In the modern technological context this formulation gives rise to the question of genocide.

Cataclysmic social and political events serve as a catalyst to ideas which are "in the air" but have not crystallized because the events have not occurred to force the reconsideration of basic conceptual frameworks, which usually set the terms of debate in international affairs. It is only now that we begin to see the direct relationship between the work of the Nuremberg judgments and a new understanding of human rights. The Nuremberg trials and judgments grew out of principles of accountability and responsibility from the laws of agency, democratic, and socialist theory. However, this conception of personal accountability and individual human rights has consistently avoided the relationship of the powers of national leaders to make war either on their own people or on people of other lands. Consequently, international law has been silent on the importance of human rights as a *line of defense* by the individual person, the family, or the community against the state's leadership and its activities as they relate to war preparations, or the more specific question of participation in warlike acts.

In this sense human rights should be seen as a condition precedent to the penumbra of policies which states follow that shade into war, cold war, arming, and covert war. It is a conceptual and moral error to assert that humanitarian rules should be found in the context of armed conflict. Instead, the "human rights" rules should be seen as governing actions of governments *precedent* to any particular policies which they intend to pursue. They are required to ask what effect the government's foreign and defense policies have on innocent populations. This question goes to the very nature of the arms acquisition and arms race process, a more euphemistic phrase for the preparation of mass murder and genocide.

The legal formulations and judgments to emerge from Nuremberg and the Asian war crimes trials, as well as the moral suasion of the Universal Declaration, the charter, and later resolutions of the General Assembly on war and disarmament, are in direct conflict with the types of weapons which states acquire or make. Besides being a horrifying tragedy, their use sets the stage for considering those who prepare, acquire, and use such weapons as criminals. In this sense, if the killing cannot be legitimated by the laws of war, then surely the actions of leaderships fall more within the context of domestic and international criminal concern than high policy. Municipal law becomes the means of bringing action against leaderships once the proper legislation is passed to bring leaderships to justice for denying the security of the person through the means of weapons chosen to defend the citizen.

Making Government Accountable

Obviously the question of bringing such actions against governments falls in the psychological area of political will coupled with existing legislation. Will is usually exercised where there is an aroused and organized citizenry which sees a means to bring such pressure to bear against its government by championing already existent principles. Such a stance, which uses an emerging consensus of international legal doctrine against the excesses of states, needs to find a double constituency: one is among diplomats and international civil servants; the other is among groups in other countries who see that their own liberties are directly tied to those people who are prepared to challenge state law that has no basis in universally accepted principles, while their challenge is legitimated and codified in UN Charter covenants, provisions, resolutions, and international law generally.

In some cases municipal legislation may not exist, and policymakers may think that because there is no law which abjures their action, they are not covered by the domestic criminal law. In this regard, the Kastenmeier Bill is a significant piece of legislation which would commence the tedious but necessary process of holding government officials in the foreign and national security policy areas personally accountable for their plans and practices. Kastenmeier's bill uses as a standard the norms laid on Germany and Japan at the end of World War II, stating that such legislation should be internalized in U.S. law. It also calls for internalizing the charter as well as other international legal strictures against war crimes. The bill is grounded on the principle that the person's security is robbed in the case of war, and fundamental human rights are therefore violated in the process.

War Preparation and Genocide

The nature of war preparation should now come under direct scrutiny. There is little doubt that a person's security and, therefore, human rights are directly violated by the nature of weaponry adopted. In modern states huge organizations enter into a series of activities on a daily basis which may not appear to be crimes or violations of anyone's rights. But in reality—once we are able to remove the conceptual blinders from our eyes—those actions are crimes in situ, crimes in being. The armaments race, given the nature of the arms made and the war plans fashioned, is criminal in nature when compared to laws of war or peace, the criminal laws of individual nations, and the Nuremberg and Asian trial standards. It would seem to fall within the framework of the first four articles of the Nuremberg charter.

Once we begin our understanding that we are living in an event of genocide which has not, thankfully, played out the final notes of civilization's götterdämmerung, we are able to evaluate an entire spectrum of negotiations and talks on arms control and disarmament from a somewhat different perspective than we usually use. The participants in the SALT talks, favoring great secrecy, eschew necessary moral, legal, and criminal questions when discussing armaments. When these talks are divorced from the fundamentally criminal nature of the weaponry or strategies under discussion, arms control talks are reduced to a narrow exercise between state representatives on the character and size of genocidal forces.

Unfortunately, the SALT talks give the appearance of legitimacy to the entire field of weapons of mass destruction because they create the mind-set among elites in the media and the universities, as well as the public as a whole, that such weapons are "needed" and that they should be considered in the card catalogues of libraries and treasury accounts under the heading of "Policy and Diplomacy" rather than "Crime and Criminal Behavior." There can be no successful discussion which is meant to comprehend the character and gravity of the weapons, and to limit and eliminate them, without that discussion *beginning* from accepted international legal principles about genocide, population safety, and the Nuremberg judgment of personal accountability of public officials to either municipal or international tribunals.

During the past several years, under the sponsorship of the International Red Cross, more than a hundred states have been negotiating a new set of rules for the laws of war which are to partially take the place of the 1949 Geneva protocols on war. The negotiators have excluded weapons of mass destruction from their rather intriguing set of talks on the ground that they are being dealt with in another forum. The critical question remains whether all weapons will be subjected to the same standards laid down in this almost successfully negotiated treaty.

If the negotiators have intentionally excluded weapons of mass destruction, then the document will end up as another cynical exercise of governmental duplicity. There is talk among members of the Department of State that it will have criminal sanctions attached to it. But the question of sanctions must also apply to weapons and their acquisition if there is to be much substantive meaning to the treaty. It is ludicrous to work out laws of war that in fact neither touch the nature of arms acquisition nor the major weapons in one's arsenal, which are criminal by nature and which are harmful to any basic human rights.

Implementing Human Rights

Some natural law philosophers argue that human rights attach to the human personality and therefore are more important than states themselves. They tend to argue that the raison d'être of the state is to promote human rights of the people; otherwise it has no positive purpose. Regardless of whether this point of view is accepted, it is time for worldwide meetings horizontally between city, neighborhood, and nongovernmental representatives of different nations to consider the substantive meaning of human rights in the context of the problems which humanity now faces.

The purpose of such a reconsideration is not to undo the painstaking work already accomplished, but exactly the opposite. It is to make clear that human rights are the inescapable ground upon which international relations exist, not in the sense that human rights become a cloak for busybody intervention and imperialism. Instead, they are to be the ground upon which nations, diplomats, statesmen, and people come to understand the essential need of rights in practice in questions concerning the international economic order, the arms race, the relations of their states to other states, and the internal rights of their own citizenry.

I would suggest an international, nongovernmental monitoring agency which permanently reported on the question of human rights violations, as defined according to the covenants and the Universal Declaration, the Nuremberg Charter, and the UN Charter. It would seek and receive information from governments, nongovernmental organizations, and individuals. It would also fashion economic standards and comment on major technological and military systems and their effect on human rights and individual and group security. It would aid groups in various countries. Human rights in this framework would assert that international economic actions must be in furtherance of aspirations which are stated in treaties and General Assembly resolutions that seek to set out a framework in such matters as disarmament and apartheid.

A major purpose of the UN declaration was to reach the mass of people and clarify their rights. But it is necessary for the people to have access to information and groups in their own countries or in other countries which will help in asserting the "right of human rights." Thus serious relationships which can develop, as outlined in the Helsinki Accords, for the protection of human rights and the establishment of a common understanding of them, will have the effect of strengthening concern and awareness of human rights questions. These groups should work to make operational the language of treaties, charters, and General Assembly resolutions. On a state level treaties and resolutions should be written with an eye to their effect on human rights and the consequences which any particular actions or series of actions would have on human rights.

I have in mind problems which are already recognized as human rights problems, whether torture in Chile or apartheid in South Africa, and problems which have not yet been conceptualized or politicized as such (environmental poisoning, uncontrolled scientific research, military developments). Such questions require a new consideration of human rights by nongovernmental organizations, the General Assembly, and the Security Council, with the purpose of finding means of binding states to declarations and resolutions while providing ways that people can successfully assert internationally accepted rights in their own respective nations.□

READINGS SUGGESTED BY THE AUTHOR:
Barnet, Richard; Raskin, Marcus G.; and Stavins, Ralph. *Washington Plans an Aggressive War*. New York: Random House, 1971.
Green, James Frederick. *The United Nations and Human Rights*. Washington, D.C.: Brookings Institution, 1956.
Horowitz, Irving Louis. *Genocide: State Power and Mass Murder*. New Brunswick, N.J.: Transaction Books, 1976.
Nagel, Thomas, ed. *War and Moral Responsibility*. Princeton, N.J.: Princeton University Press, 1974.
World Armaments and Disarmament: SIPRI Yearbook. Cambridge, Mass.: MIT Press, 1975.

FOREIGN NATIONALS AND AMERICAN LAW

DIANE EDWARDS LA VOY
Washington Office on Latin America

During the second half of 1976 widespread concern arose in Washington about the activities in the United States of foreign intelligence agencies—not of the Soviet KGB, but of the agencies of such friendly nations as South Korea (KCIA), Iran (SAVAK), and Chile (DINA). By the end of the year four separate investigations were under way in Congress, and five in the executive branch.

Attention has focused on evidence of a bold campaign by agents of the South Korean Central Intelligence Agency to buy influence through bribery of U.S. congressmen. Throughout 1977 the House Ethics Committee has been looking into alleged congressional wrongdoing. Meanwhile, the House Subcommittee on International Organizations has been studying the foreign relations implications of the Korean lobbying campaign. By September 1977 a Justice Department investigation had led to felony indictments against two Korean businessmen, allegedly agents of the KCIA.

The focus on congressional bribery overshadows another disturbing aspect of the problem: the intimidation, by foreign agents, of persons in the United States. Yet it is this aspect that best reveals the varied dimensions of the "friendly agent"* problem.

---

*The term "friendly agent" refers to members of the intelligence services of "friendly governments" and their agents—that is, any persons controlled or paid by them to perform intelligence collection or covert action. "Friendly" describes those governments with whom the United States is allied or maintaining other close supportive relations; the "friendly governments" are the repressive regimes whose agents operate outside their own country.

First, the KCIA's efforts to manipulate American society extend well beyond Capitol Hill. Bribery and intimidation of employees and advertisers have pressured Korean-American newspapers on the West Coast to follow a pro-Park line. Covert propaganda and intimidation have also affected the integrity of academic institutions. Second, the KCIA, which mushroomed overnight after the 1961 coup that brought President Park Chung-hee to power, is Park's instrument for controlling political activities in South Korea. KCIA activities abroad represent not an isolated policy, but an integral part of a repressive regime's fight to maintain power. Third, the problem is not limited to the Koreans. Iranian students at American universities are watched by SAVAK, and critics of the shah have reported receiving death threats. The assassination in Washington on September 21, 1976 of a prominent Chilean exile, and attacks abroad on other Chilean democratic leaders, support the fears of foreign dissidents that their own governments' secret police will hunt them down with impunity.

Conflicting Policy Goals

The failure to prevent the misdeeds of foreign agents is attributable in part to problems of criminal investigation and prosecution, such as the fear of victims, the diplomatic immunity of suspects, and the limited resources of local police departments. Restrictions of law, policy, and structure have combined to limit the FBI's role in this situation.

Perhaps the most important problems of all are those of normative policy. Current interpretations of U.S. national security goals, which include the protection of stable military and intelligence arrangements with South Korea, Iran, and a number of other repressive regimes, are fundamentally inconsistent with certain domestic goals: law and order, individual liberty, even constitutional government in the United States. The available evidence suggests that the operating partnership between U.S. and friendly intelligence services, which has been deemed essential to national security, seriously impedes the protection of individuals in the United States. It undermines the political will to have the laws obeyed.

The need to resolve these conflicting policy goals is part of the foreign policy dilemma confronting the Carter administration—how to maintain close relations with allies and cooperative relations with adversaries, while supporting the struggle for human rights abroad. An approach to the law enforcement and civil liberties problems posed by friendly agents, therefore, must be sought as much in the realm of foreign policy as in that of bureaucratic organization or law.

Impeding Law Enforcement

Mr. X is a law professor from a foreign country. His university has granted him a sabbatical for two years of postdoctoral study at an American university. In his legal practice he had defended critics of the government. He is not politically active in the United States, but has spoken critically about his government's policies in a graduate seminar and among friends.

Mr. X is invited to participate in a symposium on law and development at an Ivy League university. A week before the symposium he receives a call from an acquaintance, a local businessman from the same country.The businessman terms certain organizers of the symposium "agitators," and warns him against making any antigovernment statements. A few days later he receives a letter from his daughter back home. She urges him not to collaborate with exiled antigovernment activists, and suggests that she and her mother might otherwise be in danger. The letter reads as if it were dictated to her. He cancels his plans to participate in the symposium.

Mr. X does not report the threats to the local police. He doubts he could convince them that the call from the "businessman"—who he believes is an agent for his government—actually was a threat. Also, knowing that his government enjoys U.S. support, he distrusts all American officials, including the local police.

The hypothetical case of Mr. X combines several of the threads that run through the testimony of Koreans and the reports of Iranians and Chileans. According to Lee Jai Hyon, former chief cultural and information attaché and director of the KCIA in the United States, clandestine schemes included efforts "to intimidate 'uncooperative' Koreans and Korean-Americans through their families, relatives, and close friends in Korea to silence their criticism, and to make already silent ones more 'cooperative.'" Iranians cite the arrest and torture of Narmin Baraheni, niece of Reza Baraheni, a dissident poet living in the United States.

Baraheni found that everything he had said in the United States during the academic year 1972–73 had been reported to SAVAK. Professor T.C. Rhee, a Korean American, was contacted by the South Korean embassy prior to a Toronto conference on Asian studies, and was advised either to water down his anti-Park paper or not to present it. A 1975 Korean decree provides as much as seven years' imprisonment for anyone damaging the "security, national interest, or prestige" of Korea at home or abroad by criticizing the government.

The first impediment to law enforcement at the local level is the reluctance of victims to talk. Korean residents on the West Coast were reported in 1975 to be so afraid of KCIA reprisals against friends and relatives in Korea that they did not tell police that KCIA agents were extorting money from them; a similar claim was made more recently by a Korean businessman, filmed in shadow, interviewed in May 1976 on the NBC-TV program *Weekend*. Such fear undoubtedly prevents members of foreign communities from resorting to civil suits when they could establish claims under civil law.

A more fundamental problem in protecting foreign communities is that there may not be any provable violation of the law. According to Lee Jai Hyon, the "mere presence" of certain Koreans who are widely known among their countrymen in Washington as having close ties to the Korean Embassy "arouses enough fear to mute many Koreans." But even where there are explicit threats of physical harm—ones that could clearly be termed assaults—there is a problem of credibility. In many cases it would be difficult to convince anyone not acquainted with the power and brutality of the particular intelligence service that the threats are such "as to put in fear an ordinarily firm and prudent man," or that the person offering the threat is an agent of a brutal intelligence service and has a "present ability" to harm the subject.

Several agencies have reputations for torturing and killing political prisoners, seizing dissidents and potential informers—sometimes children—for interrogation. Such reputations turn mere hints and vague references to one's family or to one's own fate into sufficiently credible threats to ensure "cooperation."

The quiet, undramatic nature of most of the activity directed against the foreign groups makes it difficult to begin law enforcement. By contrast, a dramatic, highly visible crime—the bombing which killed Orlando Letelier and Ronni Moffitt—has drawn considerable resources from the Justice Department. The killing of a former official guest of the U.S. government violated a federal law. Public interest has been high, and the case has engaged the attention of two attorneys general. Recent reports indicate that the year-long investigation has made some progress, federal officials having determined that the bombing was directed either by officials of DINA or by persons acting on behalf of DINA officials.

Still another problem is the involvement of diplomatic or consular officials, who enjoy full or partial diplomatic immunity. The need for police to seek a statement from the Department of State on what standard of immunity an individual enjoys—and perhaps even a court determination—complicates the investigation of cases involving suspects who are diplomats or are under diplomatic cover.

The Departments of States and Justice have been slow to act and ineffective when doing so. The State Department's Office of Korean Affairs, which had been compiling complaints from Koreans in the United States since 1970, raised the issue of KCIA activities with Korean embassy officials frequently during 1973, and in the fall of that year the Korean ambassador was called in for a meeting with the deputy under secretary of state. Apparently as a result, the Korean government recalled the KCIA station chief in Washington; but the KCIA did not significantly reduce its activity, and the issue did not ruffle American-Korean relations.

Before last year, when the Department of Justice began a major investigation of Korean efforts to buy influence in Congress, its response to Department of State requests for investigation of Korean activities had been half-hearted. In 1971 the attorney general replied that evidence of violations by Radio Free Asia was insufficient to warrant prosecution, and in 1973 an FBI investigation confirmed that KCIA agents were harassing Korean residents, but accomplished little else.

Harassment by other friendly services has received even less U.S. government attention. On October 24, 1976 CBS's *60 Minutes* broadcast an interview in which the shah of Iran acknowledged that SAVAK agents in the United States are "checking on anybody who becomes affiliated with circles, organizations hostile to my country." Following the broadcast the Department of State conducted an inquiry (which took seventeen days from start to finish), and found no evidence of improper activity here by the Iranian government.

Korean residents regularly report new incidents of harassment and threats, and members of the antishah Iranian Students Association charged in November 1976 that harassment of their members had more than doubled in the previous year. Clearly, federal and local law enforcement authorities appear powerless to protect these foreign communities. That apparent powerlessness raises disturbing questions. Do agents from friendly nations enjoy a special status that permits them to violate American law? If so, what are the reasons? What form does the arrangement take? Who authorizes it? What can be done about it?

Federal Espionage Statutes

There are several federal statutes designed to identify and control the agents of foreign powers. The Foreign Agents Registration Act imposes criminal sanctions on any person who acts as an "agent of a foreign principal" within the United States unless he files a certified statement with the attorney general; information about expenses and propaganda activities must be provided. Another law requires registration with the Department of State for anyone, other than a diplomatic or consular officer or attaché, who acts in the United States as an agent of a foreign government.

In addition, a provision of the Campaign Finance Act makes it a crime for a foreign national to make contributions in any election for public office in the United States, and, under another act, it is a crime for an officer or employee of the United States in any branch of government to serve as agent of a foreign principal. There is also a little known law, the Espionage Registration Act, which requires registration with the attorney general of "every person who has knowledge of, or has received instruction or assignment in, the espionage, counter-espionage, or sabotage service or tactics of the government of a foreign country or of a foreign political party." However, the law might be construed to exempt agents of the friendly services from this requirement.

Of these statutes, only the first two apply to the bulk of cases in which friendly agents attempt to control the content of community newspapers, to silence visiting scholars, or covertly to plant propaganda through front organizations. Whereas the purpose of registration with the State Department is principally to clarify diplomatic ramifications, the Foreign Agents Registration Act, originally passed in 1938 and amended several times since, attempts to protect American society from foreign subversion. Its purpose is to uncover foreign covert action directed at influencing the beliefs of Americans or gaining control of American institutions. That is a difficult task in an open society. The legislation must protect the society from foreign manipulation without imposing unconstitutional restrictions on the exchange of ideas. Thus the act can address only the problem of secrecy; by requiring registration of agents and clear identification of the source of propaganda, it tries to bring foreign pressures and influences out into the open.

The first weakness of the act is that it prohibits nothing. A second weakness is its enforceability. Many complaints against foreign agents involve activity that is covert and "deniable." It is difficult to prove that an individual guilty of harassment acted as an agent of a foreign principal. Officials are reluctant to move when there is little "competent evidence"—that is, evidence that does not come from classified sources.

There are special problems in trying to prosecute an alien, particularly one linked to a vast intelligence network; when an investigation is begun the suspect leaves the country. Diplomatic immunity is a further complication. Diplomatic and consular officials are exempted from the act's registration requirements. This exemption may provide, in practice, a shield for nonexempted people as well. It is likely, for example, that official personnel direct propaganda and pressure campaigns; coordination may even occur at the embassy in Washington. The "dirty work," however, may well be left to others—aliens or U.S. citizens. The exemption for diplomats provides a cover over accounting records and other "paper trails" that might link the foreign government to the individual who actually does the dirty work. Finally, the act ignores some of the important ways in which agents exert influence: surveillance as a means of intimidation, threats, and the use of coercive influence based on the power to withhold official papers.

It appears unlikely that the weaknesses in the act can be corrected without jeopardizing the very liberties that it attempts to protect. It is necessary, however, to recognize the act's limitations as an instrument in protecting foreign communities in the United States from the activities of friendly agents.

FBI Participation in Law Enforcement

Much of the conduct attributed to foreign agents would clearly violate state criminal law, and an agent could be prosecuted without reference to any "foreign principal." Allegations against agents of SAVAK, KCIA, and DINA include bribery, forgery, extortion, burglary, assault, and even murder.

There may, however, be serious impediments to investigation. Recognizing threats as real and investigating them effectively may be beyond the capacity of local authorities and better handled by the FBI. Local police are hardly a match for agencies like KCIA and SAVAK, which exploit the diplomatic immunity of many of their operatives and enjoy the support of a bewildering variety of semiofficial organizations in this country and abroad. The FBI is a nationwide agency of vast investigative resources, and its Intelligence Division is familiar with the structure and methods of foreign intelligence services. The use of such resources could counteract the activities that now undermine the rights of members of foreign communities and thwart the enforcement of state criminal laws.

Two beliefs are widely held about the investigative jurisdiction of the FBI: that the bureau can investigate only when violations of federal law occur, and that its counterintelligence efforts are to be directed only at "hostile" agencies. The first is not quite accurate, and the second is false. These beliefs may have discouraged the use of the FBI in protecting foreign communities from friendly agents. They probably do prevent Congress and the public from looking to the FBI for assistance.

Allegations against friendly agents often involve violations of federal laws, including wiretapping, kidnapping and failure to register as a foreign agent. Even where the alleged action is not a federal crime, the difficulties of local and state law enforcement appear to justify FBI involvement under a statute that requires federal intervention where a state permits "unlawful combinations or conspiracies" to deprive "any part or class of its people" of their civil rights, thereby denying the equal protection of the laws secured by the Constitution. Federal civil rights legislation would appear to provide another basis for FBI involvement.

Still another basis for participation by the FBI in the investigation of criminal activity by foreign agents may be found in the power of the federal government to conduct foreign affairs. The "full exertion of the power" to conduct foreign affairs may require the federal government to exercise police powers. It is important to the conduct of relations with other nations that foreigners in this country not be subjected to intimidation or other harm. In the short run such actions undermine America's reputation as "land of the free"; they deprive this society of the candid views of foreign dissidents; and violence by foreign agents may trigger retaliation against Americans in the United States or abroad. More important, apparent tolerance of such conduct may have a harmful effect on future U.S. foreign relations, particularly if dissidents who were oppressed here by their governments' agents become their nations' new leaders.

Intelligence

So far the analysis has treated the activities of friendly agents as a problem of law enforcement, but the problem is one of intelligence as well. There may be circumstances where criminality cannot be shown, but where national security requires that the behavior of foreign agents be investigated and controlled. If the foreign agents represented unfriendly governments, this response would be termed "counterintelligence." The agency with primary counterintelligence responsibility within the United States is the FBI.

It is significant that there is no term for this national security intelligence function as it might relate to friendly services. This reflects the widespread, and erroneous, notion that the FBI's intelligence responsibilities are limited to "hostile" agents. In fact, the authority of the FBI never has been restricted to specific countries.

In practice, since World War II national security has been defined in terms of U.S. competition with the Soviet Union abroad and of the threat of communist subversion at home. Accordingly, the FBI has directed its intelligence activities at two kinds of targets: counterintelligence targets (activity of hostile governments in the United States) and "internal security" targets, which (as recent congressional investigations have shown) included a variety of so-called "extremist" and "subversive" groups.

The preoccupation with communism, subversion, and domestic disorder not only precluded considering friendly agents as a *counterintelligence* problem, but effectively prevented the FBI from helping investigate alleged *criminal activity* by friendly agents. This occurred in two ways. First, J. Edgar Hoover's FBI saw no need to protect people in the United States from anticommunists; indeed, groups that opposed U.S. support for oppressive governments were themselves targets of FBI surveillance and harassment. Second, the bureau's Intelligence Division was wrapped in a mystique so powerful that it constituted a shield against supervision by the attorney general and a barrier to effective coordination with the General Investigative Division. This lack of coordination continues to impede investigation.

Improving Law Enforcement

Of the impediments to protecting people in the United States from friendly agents, lack of political will—including the will to acknowledge friendly agents as a threat—is probably the most basic. Nevertheless, certain measures may be taken to improve law enforcement.

One such measure is increased coordination within the FBI between the Intelligence and General Investigative divisions. The expertise of the Intelligence Division with respect to organization, membership, and manipulative techniques of foreign intelligence agencies should be made available in criminal investigations.

There should be an interdepartmental review of U.S. policy concerning diplomatic immunity, to set clear standards. Although U.S. courts have construed diplomatic immunity narrowly by restricting it to officials who function as diplomats and are recognized as such, a lack of clarity about U.S. policy in dealing with foreign officials' claims to immunity may hamper effective law enforcement.

Legislation, or an executive order, may be needed to require that all federal departments and agencies provide the Department of Justice with any information they have concerning foreign agents in the United States. The Department of Justice investigation of Korean activities has apparently been slowed both by the intelligence agencies' broad application of the prohibition against disclosing "sources and methods," and by the "third agency rule," which prohibits one agency from transmitting intelligence which it obtained from another.

Clearly local police departments are no match for organizations like KCIA and SAVAK; federal involvement is needed. However, greater FBI involvement in protecting society may not be desirable. Protecting society from manipulation by agents of a "foreign ideology"—communism—was the banner under which the FBI and other agencies mounted their grotesque domestic intelligence programs. There is little likelihood of another such gross, illegal campaign, this time directed at friendly agents. The important point is that "subversion"—whether allegedly directed by the Kremlin or by the KCIA—is not easily rooted out in an open society. Neither law enforcement, nor its "domestic security" variants, can provide the full answer to the problem posed by friendly agents.

There is need for greater recognition that the oppressiveness of certain friendly governments inevitably extends into the United States. From the standpoint of domestic security and welfare, friendly agents can be as harmful as hostile agents; and they are more insidious because of the friendly environment in which they operate. Protecting people in the United States from them can be achieved only by changing that environment—whatever approval, protection, or cooperation is accorded to the illegal activities of friendly agents must be ended.

Liaison Relations

Cooperation between intelligence services is an integral part of U.S. relations with many countries. "Liaison relations" between the CIA and foreign intelligence agencies, collaboration between the military intelligence services and their foreign counterparts, and mutual assistance in some areas of criminal law enforcement are parts of the network of cooperative relationships that the United States maintains with its allies and client states. Cooperation in intelligence usually takes place in the context of military alliances and other major treaty arrangements, or of military assistance and training programs.

The purpose of the CIA's liaison relations is to exchange information, to mount joint operations against "hard" Soviet or Chinese targets or local subversives, and to penetrate foreign intelligence services. In its final report the Senate Select Committee to Study Governmental Affairs with Respect to Intelligence (the Church Committee) described liaison arrangements as "an extremely important and delicate source of intelligence and operational support."

Special Status for Friendly Agents?

The governments whose agents intimidate people in the United States are repressive at home. The way the U.S. government has responded to the human rights issue in those countries has influenced the effectiveness of efforts to protect people in the United States from the friendly agents. For example, efforts by State Department officials to press the Korean embassy to stop KCIA harassment can only have been seriously undercut by the "hands off" policy of Secretary of State Kissinger. Ambassador Popper in Chile was admonished by Kissinger to "cut out the political science lectures" in his discussions with the Chilean junta. A 1973 cable from Ambassador Richard Helms in Iran indicates that the Department of State had been considering ways to suppress an antishah newspaper published in Washington, but that department lawyers, however, "had concluded that under U.S. laws there was regrettably no basis" for closing it down.

If friendly agents do enjoy a special status that allows them to conduct surveillance, and to harass and manipulate people in the United States, the desire to maintain good relations with strategically important allies may be a reason. Iran and Korea are two such countries. The early gestures of the Carter administration in proposing cuts in military aid to Argentina, Uruguay, and Ethiopia because of human rights violations underlined the transcendant strategic importance of certain other friendly countries. Testifying in the Senate, Secretary of State Vance noted that no cuts had been recommended for Korea despite "great concern about the human rights situation there." No mention was made of Iran.

Another factor, more a matter of human nature than of considered policy, may underlie U.S. failure to crack down on friendly agents. That factor is the attitude of U.S. officials toward the foreign dissidents. When officials deal only with the regime in power (its opponents being in prison or otherwise silenced), and actively support that regime against foreign threats and internal "subversion," they tend to function according to the simple rule, "your enemy is my enemy." There is a natural tendency among U.S. intelligence officers to adopt the perspective of the local officials with whom they work closely. The network of cooperative relations that the United States maintains with friendly countries creates bonds between U.S. and foreign officials at many levels, and these bonds tend to promote common attitudes.

U.S. training and other routine contacts are intended to influence the attitudes of foreign officials—to reinforce their anticommunism, for example; but that process works both ways, and U.S. officials are influenced in turn by these contacts. Thus the U.S. intelligence community may come to view foreign dissidents living in the United States as undesirable and potentially subversive, and that attitude may lead to turning a "blind eye" to actions of friendly agents against them.

A third explanation may be that the intelligence community has opposed action against friendly agents here in order not to jeopardize intelligence activities in friendly countries. Very little is known about the form of liaison agreements, but it is reasonable to infer that any arrangement granting U.S. intelligence services certain privileges in another country would at least imply similar privileges for the other country's intelligence operations. If this reciprocity does exist, it probably has not been put in writing. More likely, it is an unstated assumption deriving from the patronal relationship the United States has with the intelligence branches of friendly governments in the Third World. In any case, the United States may be secretly granting to foreign agents the same license to break laws that U.S. agents exercise in friendly countries.

Liaison Agreements

Because of the probable link between U.S. policy toward friendly agents here and the liaison arrangements the United States has overseas, it is worthwhile to examine what is known about liaison agreements—their form, content, authority, and congressional oversight.

Very little is known about the agreements that arrange for cooperation between U.S. intelligence agencies and those of other countries. From what little has been made public about them, one would expect that the agreements set out each nation's obligations for collecting and sharing intelligence and protecting each other's intelligence sources and methods, and, where applicable, intelligence facilities. Some countries may set limits on the number of agents each country will allow.

It is not known under what authority liaison agreements are made. Nor is it known at what level of government they are negotiated and approved. What little is known, however, raises two important constitutional questions concerning the separation of powers. Does the president have the authority to conclude such agreements? What should be the role of the Congress in overseeing such agreements and in approving or disapproving them?

Although the participation of the Senate is required to ratify treaties, it is generally agreed that the Constitution permits certain treaties—called executive agreements—that do not require Senate approval. It is unclear, however, whether liaison agreements fall under the sole authority of the president as commander-in-chief; whether the president may conclude them under congressional authority pursuant to treaty (peace treaties, agreements to furnish military aid, and so on); or whether, in fact, the executive lacks the authority to conclude liaison agreements without Senate approval.

In recent years the Congress has made several efforts to define national commitments, to insist on congressional participation in making them, and to demand full reporting by the executive of all agreements. The Case (or Case-Zablocki) Act, enacted in 1972, requires the secretary of state to transmit to the Congress the text of any international agreement, other than a treaty, to which the United States becomes a party. Although the act makes provisions for preventing public disclosure of secret agreements, no intelligence agreements were sent to the Congress under it until January 1977. Considerable uncertainty on what constitutes an international agreement has hampered implementation of the Case Act in all areas; it addition, reporting of intelligence agreements has encountered resistance within the agencies.

Congressional Oversight

Even if the Case Act were strengthened and enforced to ensure that all agreements were sent to the Congress, it would still be difficult to achieve congressional oversight of the intelligence dimension of foreign relations. Intelligence agencies determined to avoid oversight can make oral agreements and other informal arrangements. Indeed, it is likely that current liaison arrangements are based as much on tacit understandings as on written agreements. More important, congressional oversight of secret activities suffers from an inherent weakness. A member of Congress derives power from the public, and from the ability to represent and mobilize public opinion on particular matters. Where oversight must be conducted in secret, this power is severely limited. Despite these limitations, however, Congress can involve itself constructively in resolving the problems posed by friendly agents in the United States.

First, Congress should investigate the activities of foreign agents in this country. Congressional hearings would serve notice on friendly nations of a commitment to protect persons here not only from the more dramatic and visible crimes of their agents, but also from subtler, more widespread efforts to intimidate and manipulate. The hearings and other expressions of continuing congressional concern should lead to the new legal authority and increased resources needed to enforce that commitment.

Second, Congress must inform itself about U.S. ties with friendly agencies. Members of the Senate and House Intelligence committees, who are aware of the needs and practices of U.S. agencies, should note any correlation between U.S. intelligence activity overseas and the indulgence of friendly agents at home. Congress should make vigorous use of the Case Act to examine intelligence agreements and working arrangements in the context of overall U.S. relations with friendly countries.

Finally, both Congress and the executive must recognize that the friendly agents problem is rooted in U.S. relations with friendly governments and cannot be eliminated without the risk of alienating or weakening those regimes. Dealing seriously with this problem will require a reorientation of U.S. policy in some regions of the world—on a scale no administration could undertake without substantial support from the Congress.

There is another fundamental challenge to current national security assumptions involved here. Freeing American society from manipulation by foreign agents may be impossible as long as U.S. policy requires maintaining the capacity to conduct covert action in other countries. A thorough reevaluation of U.S. intelligence policy, like a general reorientation in foreign policy, requires congressional participation.

Immediate steps to deal with the foreign relations side of the friendly agent problem must address two tasks. First, the U.S. government must express its determination to oppose illegal activities in the United States. The State Department should limit the number of foreign intelligence agents it will accredit, should ascertain that they are bona fide intelligence analysts, and should insist that they be assigned only to the embassy in Washington—not to consultates across the country. When investigation confirms a pattern of harassment and intimidation, the secretary of state should protest in person, and the foreign station chief under whose tenure violations of U.S. law occur should be declared persona non grata.

Second, the United States must enforce limits on the kind of cooperation that its agencies engage in with their foreign counterparts. U.S. intelligence agencies should not assist in the suppression of political opposition to the friendly regime, nor aid in any effort to violate the rights of people in the United States.

Foreign Policy Shield

Available information about friendly agents in the United States indicates that the problem of controlling their activity lies largely in U.S. relations with the friendly governments. It is as much a foreign policy problem as one of domestic law enforcement. However, the domestic importance of the problem should not be overlooked. Failure to enforce the rights of any group in the United States in principle jeopardizes the rights of the rest of society. The possible existence of secret international agreements that bear on those rights contradicts the foundation of constitutional government: the principle that laws must be public.

More energetic law enforcement is needed in order to deal with the particular difficulties of protecting foreign communities in the United States from intimidation and manipulation. But analysis of the problem reveals that the ability of an open society to protect itself from foreign manipulations is limited. Fighting "subversion"—whatever the source—can result in violating the very principles ostensibly protected.

The abuses by foreign agents appear to occur under the shield of U.S.

relations with other countries. Thus the first place to seek solutions is in those international relations.□

READINGS SUGGESTED BY THE AUTHOR:

Stanger, Roland J., ed. *Essays on Espionage and International Law*. Columbus, Ohio: Ohio State University Press, 1962.

U.S. House of Representatives. Committee on International Relations. Subcommittee on International Organizations. *Activities of the Korean Central Intelligence Agency in the United States*. Hearings, March, June, September 1976, Parts I and II.

U.S. Senate. Final Report, April 1976. *Foreign and Military Intelligence* (Book I) and *Intelligence Activities and the Rights of Americans* (Book II).

U.S. Senate. Select Committee to Study Governmental Operations with Respect to Intelligence Activities. *Intelligence Activities*. Hearings, November-December 1975. *Federal Bureau of Investigation* (Volume VI) and *Covert Action* (Volume VII).

WHY ILLEGAL MIGRATION?
A Human Rights Perspective

ALEJANDRO PORTES
Duke University

The very magnitude of contemporary illegal immigration into the United States offers sufficient cause for attention by both officials and scholars. However, the truly intriguing aspect is that such movement is anything but inevitable. For those willing to take social institutions and legal pronouncements at face value, the presence of millions of illegal workers in the country at present poses a clear paradox: on the one hand, this presence amounts to a massive violation of criminal law and is regarded as detrimental to both the nation's economy and the credibility of its institutions; on the other, illegal migration could be prevented through the adoption of technically feasible means. Why has it then been permitted?

Control of entry is in the hands of specialized enforcement agencies, especially the Border Patrol and the Investigations Division of the Immigration and Naturalization Service (INS). Both agencies have been chronically understaffed during the last two decades. In 1976 the Border Patrol had a 2,013-man force; the Investigations Divisions had 924. This enforcement personnel is supposed to guard the 1,800-mile open border with Mexico plus root out illegals in the rest of the country. Repeated attempts to increase the manpower of INS enforcement divisions have met with repeated failure in Congress, given the solid opposition of large regional blocks. A recent study conducted among illegal immigrant workers in their places of origin in Mexico concluded that "crossing the border and evading the INS is the easiest part of the migration experience."

There is consensus among all experts that inability to cope with the illegal flow is due less to technical impossibility than to political constraint. The well-known experiences of massive deportations to Mexico during the depression and of the so-called "Operation Wetback" in 1954 furnish proof that, when necessary, the movement can be reversed. The same point is documented by several recent studies of Border Patrol deployment practices. Its already scant manpower is deployed in ways which minimize interference with agribusiness in the border region. Raids are timed to avoid harvests and other peak periods of labor demand. Linewatch duty is allocated a much larger proportion of officer time than checks on farms and ranches, though the latter is the most effective means for locating illegals.

Once the thin enforcement line is bypassed, the illegal immigrant encounters few institutional obstacles in his way to employment. Social Security cards are obtained easily and employers face no penalties in making use of this cheaper source of labor. In a country where the legal status of so many individual claims is routinely subject to rapid and efficient cross-checks, it is indeed remarkable how loosely illegal immigrants are supervised by the many bureaucracies concerned with the problem.

The dilemma of illegal immigration is that, while denounced on the one hand as a national calamity, it is permitted to continue. More effective enforcement and a drastic reduction in the incentives for illegal crossing could be accomplished by fiscally feasible decisions. No such serious effort has been attempted. Constraints to initiate them have been—at least on the surface—political, and have involved several levels and branches of the state.

Conjunctural Argument

It is quite clear that continuation of illegal immigration despite its apparent costs benefits sectors of agricultural and nonagricultural employers in certain regions of the country. Reasons why these employers want to hire illegal labor are as transparent as those that propel illegals to come in the first place. Employers benefit from the lower wages, longer hours, lesser alternative opportunities, and overall greater degree of exploitation which can be imposed on illegal workers. The latter come because, relative to the permanent unemployment and underemployment and abysmal wage levels in their countries of origin, economic rewards in the United States are attractive.

Such facts have led some to interpret the movement as due to the political power of certain groups which manage to block all attempts at governmental regulation. Though true on the surface, this interpretation is limited since it likens the causes of illegal migration to a "cornering of the market" by a strategically located group. This view suggests that the phenomenon is conjunctural, since it is linked to the political stranglehold exercised by a particular

TABLE 1
Unemployment Rates and Annual Illegal Immigration, 1970–77

	U.S. Labor Force Unemployed* %	Unemployment: Change from Previous Year %	Illegal Aliens Apprehended	Illegal Aliens: Change from Previous Year %
1970	4.9	—	345,353	—
1971	5.9	+20.4	420,126	+21.6
1972	5.6	− 5.0	505,949	+20.4
1973	4.9	−12.5	655,968	+29.6
1974	5.6	+14.3	788,145	+20.2
1975	8.5	+51.8	766,600	− 2.7
1976	7.7	− 9.4	875,915	+14.5
1977	7.1†	− 7.8	1,017,000‡	

*As percent of the civilian labor force.
†First ten months' average.
‡Preliminary estimate.

Sources: Immigration and Naturalization Service (1975, 1976, 1977); U.S. Department of Labor (1976, 1977); New York Times (1977).

group against the better interests of the society. The imbalance thus caused would be solvable through organization of the opposing forces and a straightforward power play at the level of the polity.

There is evidence, however, that illegal immigration has much more deep-seated causes than what this interpretation indicates. The view that the phenomenon is conjunctural and due only to the political power of a particular interest group is contradicted by a series of facts, three of which deserve mention.

First, the government of the United States has repeatedly refused in the past to consider proposals by the government of Mexico to reinstate, in some form, the original "bracero" program. Such refusal occurs despite the fact that the very same interests benefiting from illegal migration—especially agricultural owners in the Southwest—have repeatedly and vigorously defended continuation of the program. Though somewhat more expensive than illegal labor, braceros would fulfill essentially the same economic function while providing the government with the "clear" benefits of strict regulation.

Second, despite an initially constant and then increasing rate of unemployment during the 1970s, no decisive measures have been taken by the government to prevent or slow down the rate of illegal immigration. Table 1 presents the annual rate of unemployment in the United States in recent years in comparison with the annual numbers of illegal aliens apprehended. In the absence of drastic increases in enforcement manpower or in the efficiency of procedures employed, the figure of illegal apprehensions stands as a proxy for the size of the illegal flow. Assuming a conservative ratio of one successful entry for every apprehension, illegal migration is seen to increase substantially from year to year, despite a relatively constant rate of unemployment during the early seventies.

The partial slowdown of illegal immigration during 1975 reflects the severity of the recession and not the application of new restrictive governmental policies. In relative terms, the reduction of illegal immigration during 1975 was only of 2.7 percent, despite a relative increase in unemployment of 52 percent during the year. Modest reductions in unemployment during 1976 and 1977 have been accompanied by a vigorous resurgence of illegal immigration which, according to the apprehensions estimate, passed the 1 million mark in 1977. Domestic unemployment and the illegal population have had, according to all available evidence, only a very weak inverse relationship during recent years. This occurs despite the fact that rising unemployment furnished a theoretically ideal opportunity to put pressure on interest groups hiring illegal labor.

Third, and most important, the very size and growing structural diversity of the illegal labor force makes untenable its description as a conjunctural phenomenon. A paper by Secretary of Labor Ray Marshall estimated that illegals comprised 20 percent of the increase in the U.S. labor force between 1963 and 1973. Of the 10–12 million illegal immigrants in the United States, three-fourths are estimated to have joined the labor force. If such figures can be given any credence, there are more illegal workers in the United States at present than legal immigrant workers in all of Western Europe.

In addition, it is increasingly clear that the participation of illegal workers in the labor force is not limited to agriculture. The INS estimates that one-third of the illegal aliens from Mexico are employed in agriculture; another one-third are in other goods-producing industries (meatpacking, automaking, and construction); and one-third are in service jobs. A recent survey of 628 apprehended illegals found that over 75 percent were employed in the United States in urban blue-collar and service occupations, as opposed to only 16 percent employed in agriculture.

The size of the illegal population and its growing presence in different sectors of the economy render implausible interpretations of illegal immigration as a conjunctural effect of the interests of a single politico-economic bloc. An alternative and more encompassing explanation must be sought.

Immigrants and the Labor Market

Illegal immigrant workers are, first of all, *immigrants* and, second, *illegals*. The first step in the analysis thus consists of reexamining the historical role of immigrant workers in the United States and elsewhere. The most commonly cited function of immigrant labor is to serve as a supplement to native labor. Immigrants come, according to this version, because there is not enough manpower at home to fill the needs of the economy.

If the sole role of contemporary immigration were to supplement the labor pool of industrial nations, we would expect first, that it would emerge only on conditions of full employment; second, that it would be numerically restricted—a mere fraction of the domestic labor pool; and third, that it would be highly responsive to the ups and downs of the economy so that a strong inverse correlation would obtain between periods of recession and unemployment and the reduction of the movement.

None of these conditions are satisfied by illegal immigration to the United States, as, in fact, they are not by "contract" immigration to the industrial countries of Western Europe. In both cases immigrant labor exists side by side with domestic unemployment; it is of a magnitude negating every definition as a supplementary phenomenon, and, in the long run, is poorly correlated and even tends to increase independent of domestic unemployment.

The present situation is more closely related to the true historical function of immigrant labor under capitalism, which is to protect the rate of profit. The rate of profit is fundamentally dependent on the productivity and costs of labor. Historically, the functions of immigration for capitalist expansion have been related to its providing a cheaper and more productive source of labor. The relevant literature has documented several points:

- Immigrants tend to form the part of the labor force which receives the lowest wages.
- Immigrants tend to work in the worst health and safety conditions, thereby providing for considerable "fringe" savings in the work infrastructure.
- Immigrants, contrary to general opinion, are among the healthiest and youngest workers, either because of self-selection or deliberate policy, a fact which permits greater exploitation in the form of longer hours or more intense labor.
- For the receiving economy as a whole, immigration saves the costs of rearing the worker and supporting him during early unproductive years with beneficial consequences for the overall rate of profit. To the extent that immigrants can be returned to their original countries, the economy also saves the cost of maintaining them in their late, unproductive years.
- Immigrant workers not only receive lower wages, but also affect the overall wage level since they add substantially to the available supply of labor and, hence, weaken its bargaining power.
- Immigrants also tend to weaken the internal solidarity of labor groups. This is so first, because immigrants have proven traditionally reluctant to join protracted strikes and long-term confrontations; and second, because racial and cultural differences and ensuing hostilities between immigrant and native workers tend to obscure perception of their common economic interests.

Immigrants are exploited not because they are more willing, but because they are more vulnerable; and this vulnerability is based precisely on their legal-political status. It is not only that immigrant workers are less inclined to protest, but that their rights to do so are limited by the tenuousness of their legal position. It is relatively easy to dispose of "radical" immigrants through deportation, as was the case in the United States during the early twentieth century and despite the fact that most such accusations were unfounded.

The vulnerability of immigrants is thus not based on the nature of their work performance or strictly economic position, but on the fact of having been transported (or having transported themselves) across a political border, a fact which automatically decreases their claim to the value of their product. Because of objective vulnerability, it is difficult to organize immigrant workers along lines corresponding to their economic position in the host society. Such lack of organization contributes to perpetuate their condition of defenselessness, since the employers and the state can continue to confront them as individuals rather than as a collective unit.

To be stressed is that functions of immigration in relation to the overall rate of profit depend, fundamentally, on the possibility of disposing of migrants at the point when they cease to be necessary and/or threaten to organize for demand making. The more immigrants acquire a legitimate foothold in the host society, the less advantageous their presence is and the more they come to resemble the native proletariat. Conversely, the more they can be kept at the political fringes of the society, the more useful they are in fulfilling significant functions for the economy.

Cutting Labor Costs

The need for immigrant labor and the possibilities of its fulfilling the functions detailed above depend on the political and economic context in which it exists. As a general principle, the need for foreign workers decreases when two conditions are simultaneously present: there is an abundant internal supply of labor, and the conditions for employment of domestic workers and the cost of their labor are flexible. With either condition absent, the tendency is toward an upward pressure on wages and concomitant reduction in the rate of profit.

Domestic labor inelasticity does not require a condition of full employment, for it can be created by the strengthening of working-class organizations. This is the situation most closely represented at present by the United Kingdom and the United States. Despite the theoretical availability of a reserve army of the unemployed in both countries, conditions for their free employment are limited—first by direct constraints imposed by trade unions and, second by the indirect baseline on wages provided by welfare legislation.

In general, the stronger and more widespread the organizations of the working class and the more effective their political efforts, the greater the distance between subsistence and the effective minimum salary at which domestic unemployed labor can be tapped. It is this trend which negates casual assertions by public officials that elimination of immigrant labor would automatically open up employment for citizens. Many such jobs could not exist, at least at their present wage levels, were not immigrant workers available to perform them.

Alternatives available to a capitalist economy to cope with inelasticity in the supply of labor are not limited to importation of foreign labor. The United States has been historically a country of scarce labor, and this has provided recurrent impulses for technological innovation and a capital-intensive pattern of development.

Instead of importing labor, an industry can also export itself to where available sources of cheap labor exist. Roughly 20 percent of all American investment in manufacturing in the late 1960s went abroad. Much of the rapid industrial development of places like Korea, Singapore, and Taiwan in recent years has been of this type. The rapid growth of the "maquiladoras"—U.S. industries which settle on the Mexican side of the border under a custom-and-tax agreement with the Mexican government—provide another instance of this strategy.

Not all enterprises, however, can take advantage of these alternatives. Technological development and the purchase of labor-saving equipment require large capital outlays, frequently out of reach of competitive enterprises. Similarly, the strategy of exporting the production process to less developed countries has only been implemented by large multinational corporations. Such decisions require intensive prior knowledge of the country, its labor supply, and the capacity of the local government to police its own population in defense of the interests of the enterprise.

The central point is that the alternative represented by immigration has varying functions for different layers of the capitalist economy. The largest enterprises—usually multinational ones—have at their command the devices represented by technological development and access to the peripheral capitalist countries to cope with labor restrictions. At lower levels, smaller firms lack access to alternatives for coping with increasing costs of labor. In this situation many may come to depend on immigrant workers as their means for survival. The construction industry in several countries of Western Europe furnishes a case in point.

In the United States the best known and best publicized case of dependence of enterprises on immigrant labor has been that of agricultural growers in the Southwest. But, as seen above, only a fraction of the illegal immigrant labor force is now estimated to be employed in agriculture. Factories, commerces, repair shops, restaurants, and other small- and medium-sized enterprises in cities have come to progressively rely on illegal immigration as their defense against high labor costs. It is not at all surprising, given the strategic importance of these workers, that urban employers have confronted INS attempts to identify illegals with stiff resistance. In a recent INS report it was noted that "officers of the Service encountered increasing opposition as they sought to conduct inquiries at various business establishments. Investigators were often subjected to belligerent confrontations with employers."

Resolving the Paradox

The general condition of illegal immigrants in the United States (that is, as *immigrants*), has been examined. It remains now to consider the specific character of this particular population (that is, as *illegals*). The proposition derived from the above discussion is that the real economic function of illegal workers in the United States is, in essence, no different from those fulfilled by other forms of immigration—such as temporary contract labor—in other advanced industrial economies.

Yet the specific form that the tapping of labor reserves from peripheral countries has taken in the United States requires particular attention. Whereas industrialized Western European countries have chosen to channel immigrant labor through temporary legal arrangements, the United States has maintained a surreptitious flow where individual initiative is left to provide the motor for the movement and enforcement agencies are entrusted with controlling the flow and insuring its temporary character.

The specific effect of the illegal character of immigration to the United States reinforces the very conditions which make immigrant labor economically useful. As seen above, immigrant workers can be made to labor under conditions of greater exploitation not because of any intrinsic willingness, but because of a structurally determined situation of legal vulnerability. Illegal workers, in turn, represent the most vulnerable sector of immigrant labor. Their status exacerbates those very features which place immigrant workers in the worst working conditions. Illegality, in this sense, yields a more economical solution to employers than the system of legal contract labor adopted in Western Europe.

This proposition on the function of illegal immigration does not depend on assigning deliberate intentions to any particular group of actors. The illegal "solution" to the labor problem in the United States is not one that has been deliberately planned, but rather one that has evolved from a preexisting historical situation. It is the result of a progressive convergence between the historically conditioned migration from Mexico to the United States and the needs of an ever expanding number of employers.

I am not arguing that illegal migration is the only manner of solving the labor problem in agriculture and smaller urban enterprises. Alternatives exist, like the case of Western Europe documents. The point is that the present role of illegal immigration is more central than generally assumed, for it is not limited to a particular region or a particular sector of the economy. In addition, illegal labor is, from the point of view of employers, a more convenient way of handling the situation than other alternatives. For these reasons the expanding use of illegals has successfully resisted all attempts at administrative control.

It is important to note the conditions under which illegal immigration can be used as a superior alternative to legal immigrant contract labor. Such use is contingent on maintaining the flow of immigrants under a measure of control. Effects that follow from the legal vulnerability of illegals would be considerably reduced if, as a group, they could successfully defy governmental action.

From this perspective the paradox with which I started—that between the existence of an illegal movement and the technical feasibility to prevent it—acquires a new meaning. The movement exists *because* it is not impossible to control it. More specifically, if illegal immigration were not controllable at necessary points, its utility for the economy would be reduced and its long-term costs for the state increased. In this situation—an entirely hypothetical one—we would expect substantially increased budget allocations and an expanded enforcement machinery to prevent illegal entry.

This analysis of actual consequences thus helps explain a superficially puzzling situation. Illegal immigrant labor is allowed to enter precisely because it can be made not to. It is this situation which directly guarantees the insertion of the worker in the most disadvantageous terms vis-à-vis employers and, hence, aids in maintaining profitability in threatened competitive enterprises.

Scapegoating: Ideological Campaign

In essence, the fundamental cause underlying illegal migration has to do with the contemporary operations, needs, and constraints of a developed capitalist economy. The groups for which the effects of illegal immigration are both obvious and negative are located among the working class, especially among its most powerless and disorganized sectors in rural and urban areas. The groups for which effects of immigration are more implicit and positive are found among those placed in positions of economic power. There is a third, final level of analysis which concerns ideological effects which the apparent, publicly diffused negative consequences of illegal immigration have. First, public depiction of illegal immigrants as an "alien wave" of undesirables who simultaneously take jobs away from Americans and add to the welfare-supported population can hardly be said to generate feelings of solidarity toward those involved. The manifest image of illegal immigrants and the associated absence of popular legitimacy further isolate this group and increase its vulnerability.

Second, the apparent consequences of illegal migration—widely diffused by the mass media and the governmental machinery—exacerbate the hostility of domestic labor toward illegal workers. Such hostility undermines chances for a united front in defense of common interests and shifts attention from the ultimate responsibility of employers—as a class—for the existing situation. Leaders of domestic labor organizations have come to blame their difficulties on the presence of illegal workers. This attitude attacks consequences, rather than causes, of the phenomenon; it neglects the fact that the situation of illegal immigrants is not created *by* them but *for* them by the structure of economic interests in their own countries and that which receives them in the United States.

This argument stands in a relationship of fairly logical progression to the preceding ones. It was argued, first, that the effect of immigration is to maintain rates of profit by increasing the flexibility of exploitation of labor. It was argued, second, that the effect of illegality is to expand the condition of vulnerability of foreign labor by depriving it of legal rights and forcing it to avoid any externally induced attempts at protest or organization. It is argued here, finally, that the ideological consequence of the publicly acknowledged negative effects of illegal immigration is to accentuate further the defenselessness of these workers by depriving them of a basis of solidarity with the native population and converting them into objects of blame by the working class.

Denunciations of illegal immigration by the press and public officials thus function—whether by deliberate intent or not—as the ultimate means by which to render this group the most vulnerable and isolated source of labor and, hence, a most useful one in fulfilling central functions in the economy.

Migration and Human Rights

This article takes as its point of departure the apparent paradox between a situation of massive violation of the law in the presence of legal and technical means to prevent it. The discussion has thus concentrated on domestic consequences of illegal immigration. As an approach to the phenomenon, this analysis is incomplete for it does not consider conditions in the sending countries, the economic and social impact of return migrants, and, more broadly, the articulation of countries at different levels of development in an ongoing international economy. Just as illegal immigrants are seen to fit structural needs of contemporary U.S. capitalism, the movement as a whole fits logically the present situation and constraints of an evolving international order. Migrations—legal and illegal—are seen from this perspective as the human response to conditions of uneven economic development and terms of exchange between nations.

Human rights implications of the illegal flow are not difficult to tease out. Migrations under capitalism are simultaneously the way of creating and utilizing a labor force under favorable terms and the strategy of the poor to cope with constraints of their situation. The imbalance in power and gain between employers and migrant workers is inherent in the dynamics of the economic system. Illegal immigration is, in essence, an instance of criminalizing a preexisting migration flow so as to further tilt the balance in favor of employers. Illegal workers not only increase profits for the enterprises that employ them, but can be used as scapegoats to justify unemployment to the domestic working class. Once the inner workings of this situation are uncovered, it is seen to exceed even the most minimal contemporary standards of morality. Illegal migration is a crime committed against, not by, migrant workers.

The rights violated by this situation are not of the kind which have given rise to most "human rights" concerns. They are not the political rights of individual students, politicians, or intellectuals violated by police repression, but the rights of a class of workers violated by the structure of the economic order. Though less visible than middle-class political violations, the human rights involved are more basic and the violations are more numerous and more sustained in time.

The governments of the United States and Mexico have seldom been brought to the bench of the accused in international "human rights" forums. Yet it is clear that massive exploitation of illegal labor could not go on without their complicity. It is the enforcement of a political border, coupled with tacit support for continuation of the flow, which has given rise to the present situation. Overt denunciations of political violations elsewhere must, therefore, be regarded as hypocritical, until covert compliance with violations of the rights to economic fairness and social dignity by workers on both sides of the border is ended. □

READINGS SUGGESTED BY THE AUTHOR:

Bonacich, Edna. "Advanced Capitalism and Black/White Relations: A Split Labor Market Interpretation." *American Sociological Review* 41 (February 1976): 34–51.

Castells, Manuel. "Immigrant Workers and Class Struggles in Advanced Capitalism: The Western European Experience." *Politics and Society* 5 (1975): 33–66.

North, David S., and Houston, Marion F. *The Characteristics and Role of Illegal Aliens in the U.S. Labor Market: An Exploratory Study*. Washington, D.C.: Linton and Company, 1976 (mimeographed).

Stoddard, Ellwyn R. "A Conceptual Analysis of the 'Alien Invasion': Institutionalized Support of Illegal Mexican Aliens in the U.S." *International Migration Review* 10 (Summer 1976): 157–89.

Wolpe, Harold. "The Theory of Internal Colonialism: The South African Case." In *Beyond the Sociology of Development*, edited by Ivar Oxaal, Tony Barnett, and David Booth. London: Routledge and Kegan Paul, 1975.

NGOs

JAMES FREDERICK GREEN
Commission to Study the
Organization of Peace

Among the many unusual features of the United Nations Conference at San
Francisco in April-June 1945 was the presence of forty-two private organizations, in official association with the United States Delegation as "con-
sultants." This was the first time in history that citizens' groups had participated actively in an intergovernment conference. The representatives of the
forty-two nongovernmental organizations (NGOs) helped insert into the Charter of the United Nations two subjects that had not been mentioned in the earlier
Dumbarton Oaks Proposals or, for that matter, in the constitution of any
previous intergovernmental organizations.

The first of these innovations, Article 71, recognizing the need for citizen
participation, provided that the Economic and Social Council may make suitable arrangements for consultation with nongovernmental organizations, both
international and national, which are concerned with matters within its competence. The second innovation was the inclusion in the charter of seven references to human rights and fundamental freedoms. These two unprecedented
and interrelated provisions were to have a continuing impact upon the evolution
of the new organization.

The NGO representatives and a number of delegations favored the inclusion
in the charter of an "International Bill of Rights," but time did not permit the
formulation at San Francisco of so complex an instrument. That task has been a
continuing one over the past thirty-two years. Throughout the drafting of the

many international conventions concerning human rights, the nongovernmental organizations have played an active part in pressuring governments and lobbying in conference corridors.

In order to understand the relationship of nongovernmental organizations to human rights in the United Nations, it is essential to distinguish between the two kinds of rights that are set forth in international instruments—civil and political rights, on the one hand and economic, social, and cultural rights on the other. It is also essential to realize the two different kinds of implementation that are provided in these international instruments, tailoring the procedures to the kind of rights that are involved. The activities of nongovernmental organizations vary widely, therefore, with regard to the two different kinds of rights that are being promoted and protected.

Two Kinds of Rights

Throughout its pioneering efforts over the past thirty-two years to codify, promote, and protect human rights, United Nations organs have had to take account of the differing attitudes of governments about the nature of the older civil and political rights and the newer economic, social, and cultural rights. During the drafting of the Universal Declaration of Human Rights in 1946–48, the Western countries emphasized "the rights of man," long established in their tradition. They did not deny the importance of other categories of rights; indeed, they had included "freedom from want" as one of the wartime Four Freedoms, and the United States had recognized the right to work in its Full Employment Act of 1946. Both the Communist and the nonaligned countries argued that economic, social, and cultural rights were more important and more urgent. To the hungry slum dweller or tungry peasant, they asserted, the right to eat was of more immediate significance than the right to due process of law. The result was a synthesis: a document that combined the two sets of rights.

The dichotomy continued during the long effort in 1949–56 to translate the Universal Declaration into treaty form. The West reiterated its insistence that economic, social, and cultural rights were not justiciable: they could not be guaranteed by international treaty and national legislation and enforced by courts. The East, and increasingly the newly independent developing countries, argued that these rights are equally susceptible of codification. The result was another synthesis: two separate conventions, each setting forth the provisions of the Universal Declaration at greater length, more detail, and more precise legal language. The decision to draft two separate covenants recognized that the two sets of rights were equal in significance but different in character. The distinction is made clear in Article 2 of both covenants.

Whatever the objections to economic, social, and cultural rights on philosophical or legal grounds, for over three decades the United Nations has proceeded on the assumption that they are genuine human rights and are to be accorded the same dignity and urgency as civil and political rights. A comprehensive survey of these rights, their status in member states, and the role of the United Nations, the specialized agencies, and other intergovernmental organizations in promoting these rights, was published in 1975. Indeed, the continuing debates in the General Assembly over international cooperation for economic development and the formation of a new international economic order are, in a sense, a recognition of the validity of economic, social, and cultural rights.

The two sets of rights have been combined, moreover, in the reporting system established by the Economic and Social Council. State members of the United Nations and members of the specialized agencies have been invited to submit periodic reports on human rights in the territories subject to their jurisdiction within a continuing cycle. Under the current schedule governments submit reports every two years on one of the following subjects: (1) civil and political rights, (2) economic, social, and cultural rights, and (3) freedom of information. In 1975 the Ad Hoc Committee on Periodic Reports of the Commission on Human Rights considered reports received under the second category; and, in early 1977, it considered reports received under the third.

The two sets of rights are linked by the identical provision in each covenant that they are to be enjoyed without discrimination of any kind as to "race, colour, sex, language, religion, political or other opinion, national or social origin, property, birth or other status." Not only must civil and political rights be enjoyed without discrimination, a principle long accepted though not always practiced, but also economic, social, and cultural rights must be similarly enjoyed, a principle probably even more difficult to effect in practice. The promotion of economic, social, and cultural rights is therefore to be measured both quantitatively and qualitatively.

Two Forms of Implementation

Difficult as has been the process of formulating human rights in treaty form, the task of implementing those rights has been even more torturous. Governments, which violate the rights of citizens or permit their violation, do not welcome exposure and criticism of their actions. Nevertheless, the Commission on Human Rights and its Subcommission on the Prevention of Discrimination and the Protection of Minorities have been authorized to receive and examine, in private, communications from individuals and groups alleging violations of rights, and to report to the Economic and Social Council any patterns of gross and consistent violations.

The commission and subcommission conduct their reviews of complaints in secrecy, but it may be assumed that most complaints relate to civil and political rights. These two bodies have reportedly considered a number of situations, but so far they have made no reports to the council about particular countries. More progress is apparently being made at present through another procedure available to the commission and the subcommission—the studies of specific rights, based upon information supplied by governments, nongovernmental organizations, the press, and other sources.

The distinction between civil and political rights on the one hand, and economic, social, and cultural rights on the other, is manifest in the two different kinds of implementation provided in the two covenants, the International Covenant on Civil and Political Rights (ratified by forty-four states) and the International Covenant on Economic, Social, and Cultural Rights (ratified by forty-six states). Heretofore, nongovernmental organizations in consultative status with the council have been able to participate, with limitations, in the consideration by the commission of reports submitted periodically by governments on the state of various categories of rights. Under the new reporting procedure of the covenant these organizations will, it is hoped, have the same privilege.

Because of the provision in Article 2 that these rights will be exercised "without any discrimination of any kind," the nongovernmental organizations have a new opportunity to challenge governments on their observance of economic, social, and cultural rights. They would do well to focus attention on the extent to which the present forty-four states party to the covenant on civil and political rights—especially in the ten Communist countries and the authoritarian regimes in many of the twenty-six Third World countries—ensure that everyone, without discrimination of any kind, is given equal treatment in the enjoyment of the right to work, to social security, to good health, and the other rights.

Two Levels of Activity

From the San Francisco Conference onward, nongovernmental organizations have played an active part in the human rights field. They have helped draft standards in the charter and in the many subsequent international declarations and conventions and to implement the protection of human rights prescribed in those instruments. The nongovernmental organizations concerned with human rights, whether on a full-time basis or only marginally, undertake two different kinds of activities: representation at the headquarters of the United Nations and of the specialized agencies, at world conferences, and in special programs; and operations in the field.

One of the many innovations of the United Nations is the continuing relationship of many of its organs, albeit limited, with nongovernmental organizations. The League of Nations, the International Labor Organization, and other earlier agencies maintained close contact with many private groups, but on an informal basis. Today a wide variety of nongovernmental organizations monitor the work of the United Nations at the headquarters in New York and Geneva. They provide a two-way channel of communication between the organization and the public in its member states—a flow of information and interpretation both inward and outward.

The need for recognizing public participation in the new organization was provided for in Article 71 of the charter, whereby the Economic and Social Council may make arrangements for consultation with nongovernmental organizations, both international and national. The council has developed three levels of relationship. The council has also prescribed strict procedures for NGO participation in its work, and that of its functional and regional commissions, through oral and written statements. There are 688 nongovernmental organizations that now have some form of consultative status.

Some three hundred nongovernmental organizations are registered with the United Nations Office of Public Information: certain organizations that have been granted consultative status with the Economic and Social Council, and a larger number of other organizations with more general interests. Both groups receive the same services from the Secretariat's Office of Public Information and Center for Economic and Social Information—weekly briefings, regular distribution of documents, and frequent film shows. In addition, the Secretariat's Department of Economic and Social Affairs has an NGO section for liaison with the NGOs in consultative status with the council.

This outflow of information and interpretation is of great value in developing public support for the United Nations. The three hundred nongovernmental organizations associated with the Office of Public Information can reach, through national affiliates, a potential audience of 850 million people. The NGO representatives use newsletters and other modes of communication to inform their organizations, often very large, of current developments.

The inflow of information and interpretation is equally significant. The Conference of NGOs in Consultative Status has committees in New York and Geneva on development, disarmament, human rights, and the United Nations Decade for Women. In these committees NGO representatives are able to question delegates and Secretariat officials and, individually or jointly, seek to influence them through formal and informal lobbying. Most important, they have the right to submit their views, orally or in writing depending upon their status, to the council and its subsidiary bodies. In addition, NGOs with specialized interests provide background papers and technical materials to offices of the Secretariat working on particular subjects.

Spirited Opposition

The success of these nongovernmental organizations in exposing violations of civil and political rights and the consequent publicity have not been without some disadvantages. The Communist states have from the beginning been less than enthusiastic about NGO activity in the field of human rights. The more active and vocal the NGOs have become in bringing allegations before the Commission of Human Rights and its Subcommission on the Prevention of Discrimination and the Protection of Minorities, the more the Soviet Union and its allies have criticized and opposed the procedures for consultative status with the Economic and Social Council. In recent years they have been joined by many of the developing countries, whose violations of civil and political rights have been exposed by the NGOs.

In 1975 the opponents of the NGOs persuaded the commission to adopt a resolution recommending that the council warn the NGOs about indiscriminate activities and threaten to suspend the privileges of any that transgress the rules. The council somewhat softened the resolution, but the NGOs were effectively put on notice. In the council's Committee on Nongovernmental Organizations, which reviews applications for consultative status or an upgrading of status, the Soviet Union for the past several years has taken the lead in questions, criticisms, and opposition.

In the spring of 1977 the critics of the NGOs, led this time by Argentina, renewed their attack. In a resolution expressing displeasure over violations of the rules, they persuaded the council to request the NGOs to submit by October 31 a report on their UN activities over the past four years and instructed its Committee on Nongovernmental Organizations to hold a two-week session in January 1978 to review the record of all organizations in consultative status.

It is a tribute to the NGOs, however, that the General Assembly's Ad Hoc Committee on the Restructuring of the Economic and Social Sectors of the United Nations System has recommended that NGO relationships not only with the Economic and Social Council but also with organizations of the whole system and with world conferences should be improved. As a stimulus, a group of NGOs has submitted a statement noting that at each session of the General Assembly the seven committees and the plenary adopt resolutions requesting assistance from the NGOs and making detailed proposals for making that assistance more widespread and effective.

Special Consultative Status

Many other bodies within the United Nations system are also concerned with the promotion of economic, social, and cultural rights. The scope of this NGO activity is too broad and too interconnected with economic and social development in the developing countries to be discussed in detail. At least one-half of the international NGOs in consultative status with the Economic and Social Council are professional and scientific agencies, whose special interests place them in consultative status with one of the special programs of the United Nations or with one or another of the specialized agencies.

Within the United Nations itself, four special programs have proved of such interest to nongovernmental organizations that separate arrangements for consultative status have been developed by each: the United Nations Conference on Trade and Development, the United Nations Development Program, the United Nations Environmental Program, and the United Nations Children's Fund. Similar arrangements for consultative status have been devised for NGOs, many of them professional and scientific organizations, by the principal

specialized agencies concerned with economic, social, and cultural development: the Food and Agricultural Organization of the United States, the International Labor Organization, the United Nations Educational, Scientific, and
Cultural Organization, the United Nations Industrial Development Organization, and the World Health Organization.

Within the past decade a new form of NGO activity has developed: participation in world conferences on specific subjects. In addition, the nongovernmental organizations are concerned in longer-term activities, such as International
Women's Year in 1975, the Decade for the Elimination of Racial Discrimination which began in December 1973, the International Year of the Child in
1979, and the United Nations Decade for Women: Equality, Development, and
Peace, 1976–1985. World conferences were included in the first two programs,
but not in plans for the Year of the Child. Over the past three years, thanks to
contemporary communications, NGO representatives in a number of cities in
the United States, Canada, and Western Europe have been able to maintain
daily contact with their counterparts at the site of world conferences.

Field Operations

Long before the League of Nations or the United Nations came into existence, voluntary agencies—as they were called before the more precise but less
euphonious phrase, nongovernmental organizations, was invented—were active not only in their home countries in North America and Western Europe but
also in foreign areas, including the many dependent territories. Ever since
1907, the Union of International Associations at Brussels has maintained a
central registry and information service for all international organizations, both
governmental and nongovernmental. Its latest compendium, *Yearbook of International Organizations, 1974*, lists a grand total of 4,310 organizations of all
kinds, of which 373 are intergovernmental organizations. The remaining 3,937
nongovernmental organizations are divided into 24 categories.

There are at least fifty-seven varieties of nongovernmental organizations,
many of which are grouped together under international umbrella agencies.
These NGOs, both international and national, undertake a vast range of activities, mostly unpublicized except perhaps within their own memberships,
that promote economic, social, and cultural rights throughout the world,
especially in the developing countries. These activities cover such varied fields
as disaster relief, public health, population control, maternal and child health,
educational and vocational training, housing, and technical assistance of many
kinds.

Many NGOs seek through their programs to help those whose rights are in
jeopardy, such as the poor, refugees, the handicapped, women, and children.
Increasing attention is being given to the rural poor, who are often overlooked
in economic development programs, and to persons living in inaccessible areas,
remote from the goods and services available to urban dwellers. Cultural rights,

which usually are ignored in this trilogy of rights, are being promoted through programs to perpetuate handicrafts and other local cultural activities.

The transfer of resources from the developed countries to the developing countries is usually measured by the bilateral and multilateral aid provided by governments. Less publicity is given to the international aid provided by the nongovernmental organizations, totalling approximately $1 billion a year. In 1975 ninty-four nongovernmental organizations in the United States alone contributed $597 million in cash, supplies, and equipment to overseas programs.

A directory published in 1971 (with annual supplements by the American Council of Voluntary Agencies for Foreign Service) lists an astonishing total of 494 American organizations, as of 1977, that are engaged in foreign aid and technical assistance and thus promoting economic, social, and cultural rights in developing countries. These impressive sums, donated in the developed countries by millions of individuals through their voluntary agencies, in addition to the small share of their taxes devoted to foreign aid programs, is of course augmented by personal contacts and assistance offered by the headquarters and field staffs of the nongovernmental organizations.

One relatively new variety of NGO activity is the overseas volunteer programs, some sponsored by governments (like the Peace Corps initiated by the United States) and others by nongovernmental organizations, with or without official funding. By 1973 these volunteers constituted an estimated 22 percent of the nearly 100,000 technical assistance personnel serving in the developing countries.

The presence of representatives of both intergovernmental agencies and nongovernmental organizations in the same developing country, often working on identical or related problems, has created an obvious need for coordination both at headquarters and in the field. In recent years increasing effort has been made toward consultation and coordination by the United Nations and the nongovernmental organizations. These efforts have reportedly done much to remedy the lack of communication that frequently existed in a particular country between the representatives of intergovernmental organizations and those of nongovernmental organizations, and among the NGO representatives themselves.

Future Action: United Nations

Nongovernmental organizations vary so greatly in size, resources, and interests that it is impossible to offer any recommendations for future action that would be appropriate for all of them. With some hesitation, therefore, a few suggestions are outlined for action by international NGOs in the United Nations and by national NGOs in the United States.

Perhaps it would suffice to say that international NGOs represented at the United Nations—in New York, Geneva, and regional offices—should continue to do "more of the same." Many of these organizations are preoccupied with their own special interests and are only peripherally concerned with the United Nations in general and with human rights in particular. Others have become disenchanted with the United Nations in recent years because of the alleged "politicization" of the intergovernmental organizations and their actions on Middle East issues.

What is needed today is for NGOs that have lost interest or reduced activity in United Nations affairs to reverse course and give the organization the attention and support that it deserves. The Carter administration, to its credit, is reversing the official course. The NGO community should note this encouraging development, after a decade of official neglect, and should take heart from the fact that three of its ablest representatives have been appointed to high posts in the United Nations field.

In the protection of human rights, nongovernmental organizations should continue to monitor actions of governments everywhere and to report violations of freedom wherever they occur. Nongovernmental organizations and the press are the safeguards of the liberty of the citizen against his or her government. With respect to both civil and political rights and to discriminatory practices in the enjoyment of economic, social, and cultural rights, the NGOs have a major role to play. Their submissions to the Economic and Social Council, the Commission on Human Rights, and the subcommission can bring needed pressure to bear upon governments. In doing so, the NGOs must of course act with discretion and be able to document their allegations, lest their privileges be reduced, and they must deal with equal fairness with all countries.

In the promotion of human rights, perhaps the nongovernmental organizations need to give more attention to economic, social, and cultural rights. The work of the United Nations system for economic and social development is, in effect, the promotion of economic, social, and cultural rights. The NGOs can continue to encourage and assist this work at the headquarters and in the field. In particular, they can strengthen their affiliates where they exist in developing countries, and help create new ones where they do not.

Future Action: United States

National nongovernmental organizations in this country are engaged in a wide range of activities, either independently or as part of international NGOs, in both representation at headquarters and in field operations. The advent of the Carter administration, with its strong emphasis upon human rights, primarily civil and political rights at the outset, offers an unparalleled opportunity to the American NGOs to enlarge these activities. At the top of the agenda should be action to obtain U.S. adherence to the principal international conventions in this field. Here the record of the United States is poor, in contrast to that of the Communist countries and many others with authoritarian governments. The position of the United States as a champion of human rights would be enhanced if this country became a party to at least some of the principal conventions that the world community has adopted as part of international law.

The recent statements of President Carter, Secretary of State Vance, and Ambassador Young reaffirming American devotion to the cause of human rights are most welcome. New initiatives are needed on many fronts, including the recognition of the significance of economic, social, and cultural rights. American adherence to the principal international conventions about human rights would be one valuable demonstration that this country wishes its devotion to human rights to be translated into law and into action.□

READINGS SUGGESTED BY THE AUTHOR:

Commission to Study the Organization of Peace. *Some Aspects of the International Protection of Human Rights*. New York: Commission to Study the Organization of Peace, 1977.

Green, James Frederick. *The United Nations and Human Rights*. Washington, D.C.: Brookings Institution, 1956.

United Nations. *The United Nations and Human Rights*. New York: United Nations, 1973.

Van Dyke, Vernon. *Human Rights, the United States, and World Community*. New York: Oxford University Press, 1970.

Weissbrodt, David. "The Role of International Nongovernmental Organizations in the Implementation of Human Rights." *Texas International Law Journal* 12 (Spring/Summer 1977): 293–320.

HUMAN RIGHTS AS AN
INTERNATIONAL LEAGUE

LAURIE S. WISEBERG and HARRY M. SCOBLE
University of Illinois at Chicago Circle

The year 1976 was not only the Bicentennial celebration of the United States of America. In certain respects the year also marked the celebration of effective demands for human dignity—demands sharply articulated during the American and French revolutions and still reverberating.

From the perspective of social scientists, a major issue posed by this fact is that of substance or shadow: does this development represent genuine growth in the valuation of human dignity or does it merely reflect the trendy, faddish "radical chic" of American liberals? Stated differently, are human rights finally high on the agenda of U.S. public and private policymakers and likely to be an enduring feature of American politics?

Anatomy of the League

The International League for Human Rights (ILHR) is a nongovernmental, nonpartisan, political organization: it has never knowingly received money from any government, nor has any government funded its projects. Supported wholly through voluntary contribution, the league has essentially two categories of members: contributing members (of whom there are about 2,000)

From "The International League for Human Rights: The Strategy of a Human Rights NGO" by Laurie S. Wiseberg and Harry M. Scoble. Copyright © 1977 by the *Georgia Journal of International and Comparative Law*.

each of whom pays an annual $10 membership fee; and affiliate members, human rights groups around the world (of which there are now thirty-eight) whose affiliation with the league has been approved by the ILHR's Board of Directors, and which may, though they are not obliged to, financially support league activities. Until the late 1960s the league operated on a tiny budget ($15,000 in 1967), and it was only after it received a bequest of $100,000 in 1968 that the league hired a full-time executive director and expanded its budget to $40,000. Currently the league operates with a regular budget of about $50,000; additional special expenses—for example, to send league observers on foreign missions—are covered by special fund-raising events.

In many respects the ILHR was initially patterned on the model of the early American Civil Liberties Union (ACLU). Both organizations were strongly influenced by the dynamic personality of Roger Nash Baldwin. The ACLU was deliberately created and maintained—at least until after World War II—as a small, private, informally organized staff organization. This accorded with Roger Baldwin's social philosophy and operational ideology, drawn from nineteenth century concepts of noblesse oblige and private charitable service, influenced no doubt by Baldwin's early career as a social worker in Saint Louis.

Recruitment was mainly by an "old-boy" network of those known to, and trusted by, those already in the organization; the emphasis was on discreet and indirect political action, by an exclusive focus on and single-minded faith in the efficacy of the federal judicial process. "Members" existed solely to supply financial contributions to sustain the professional activities of the legal staff. In like manner, the league was also maintained as a small, private, very informally organized and almost "social" group.

This early form that the ILHR assumed has both advantages and disadvantages. As to the former, the method of recruitment ensures that an underlying consensus is built into the organization; and this minimization of conflict (both between leadership and membership and within the leadership elite) permits organizational flexibility and speed in decision making. However, a political interest group based upon this model suffers important disabilities, the main one being a lack of resources. That is, to be effective an interest group generally requires either mass membership or money (which often can serve as a substitute for sheer numbers). Influence may, of course, derive from the skills and high status of the membership—which in fact were the resources with which the early league achieved its positive law-making successes; yet these resources can carry a group only so far.

If our assessment is correct—that the problem of human rights has shifted away from legislation to the sphere of implementation, and if national governments are the key to solving the problem of implementation (that is, in the final analysis human rights are protected or violated by national legislation and the behavior of national elites)—then a political group which consciously remains small, informal, and private forfeits the opportunity for maximal political effectiveness. It is precisely this problem that the league began to confront in the late 1960s with the expansion of its budget, the appointment of full-time paid staff, the numerical increase and elaboration of its Board of Directors and its International Advisory Committee, and experimentation with new strategies of action.

Unique Feature

In terms of anatomical structure there is, however, a unique feature to the International League which has significantly conditioned the search for relevant and effective strategies: in contradistinction to other human rights non-governmental organizations (NGOs), at one level the league is a confederation of functioning national civil libertarian organizations. Thus Baldwin's desire to create civil liberties interest groups (patterned on the ACLU model) abroad was readily manifested in league activities; Baldwin personally helped establish such groups in Japan, Germany, and Korea after World War II, with the support of the U.S. government.

Over the thirty-odd years of its existence, the *international* quality of the league has derived not merely from its objective in elaborating a corpus of international human rights law, but especially from its aspiration to help create and sustain functioning effective civil liberties organizations in national societies. Therefore, league affiliates are not just chapters or sections of the league in diverse countries; the thirty-eight league affiliates are (at least theoretically) established civil liberties groups working to further human rights in their own societies. League support for these affiliates is a clear reflection of its belief that the principal protection of human rights must come through the effective implementation of national law: national legislation must be brought into line with international human rights standards.

Organizational Structure and Affiliates

Theory and practice are not always, of course, consonant, and an examination of the league's affiliates raises questions about organizational ideology and rhetoric. That is, the league affiliates constitute something of a "hodge-podge" of diverse groups and diverse relations with the ILHR. A few—like the ACLU, the Irish Association of Civil Liberty, or the Canadian Civil Liberties Association—clearly fit the criteria of nongovernmental, human rights, activist organizations oriented toward extending and protecting civil liberties in their own countries; but others are less clearly so categorized.

The problem of the league's affiliates can be approached from a somewhat different angle. If one considers their geographic distribution, there is a highly skewed representation: eight are North American, twelve are Western European, two are Latin American, two are African, one is Middle Eastern, and the Asian groups are largely in the Western capitalist sphere. There is only one league affiliate from the Communist world. What this implies, at least indirectly, is that the league has not been highly successful in its early objective of trying to stimulate the creation of civil liberties groups abroad.

Hence, to explain the Western bias in both the geographic and political-regime distribution of its affiliates, the league must admit that few nongovernmental human rights groups exist in either Third World or Communist countries. Sometimes they exist as opposition groups in exile; but the league has understandably been reluctant to affiliate such groups for fear that they will draw the league directly into the partisan politics of other states. Hence, even relaxing the criteria for affiliate status—and, of course, it should be noted that the league does not possess any investigatory means for testing whether applicant groups really are nongovernmental, actively functioning, and pro-human rights—the biases in league affiliates are glaring.

What this reflects most clearly is the difficulty the league has faced trying to be both an American organization and an international coalition. Outside Western or Western-oriented countries, interest group structures have not been elaborated in the American fashion. This is, to some extent, compensated for by an informal mechanism whereby the league accepts "correspondents" in countries where it does not have affiliates. However, while this provides the league with access to information on events and developments in "closed" societies, this is not the same as having an organizational affiliate link.

One final point should be noted about the league structure. In the league's annual reports, in its statements and special studies, and in the composition of its Board of Directors and International Advisory Committee, the league could generally be characterized as "Western/liberal" in terms of ideology. Neither its membership nor its officers reflect one partisan political philosophy or one professional occupational category, although both its membership and support clearly derive from the educated, scientific/professional/artistic middle and upper strata of society, with the time and discretionary income to devote to international politics.

That is, while the league frequently takes up the cause of "the oppressed masses," the league is itself an elite organization. It is neither "mass membership," nor does it seek to be a radical leader of the mass. Additionally, while the effect of the league's successful interventions is to preserve the possibility for the emergence of a genuine counterelite, the league itself is not that counterelite.

New Strategies

In the 1973 annual report of the International League its new (and present) chairman, Jerome J. Shestack, assessed the first twenty-five years' experience with the Universal Declaration in somber terms. Against this background, the league began to reassess its primary strategy of focusing on the United Nations as its main political arena. Thus the league has been involved in a major reappraisal of the UN as principal forum for human rights.

In terms of organizational biography, disillusionment with the United Nations and the former league focus on law making coincided with the elaboration of the organizational structure, increase in the budget, and expansion of the Board of Directors of the league. Thus, in the early 1970s, the ILHR became concerned with defining for itself a new role in effective human rights implementation as well as differentiating itself from other human rights NGOs. As Roberta Cohen, executive director of the league, has characterized the process, the organization has been engaged in a search for a new methodology.

One of the first attempts to engage in more meaningful and innovative activism grew out of the existing league strategy of supporting national-level affiliates. In June 1971 the Board of Directors of the ILHR, after intense debate, took the unprecedented step of affiliating with a Soviet organization. The Moscow Human Rights Committee was founded in November 1970 by three Russian scientists—Andrei D. Sakharov, A.N. Tverdokhlebov, and V.N. Chalidze. These were later joined by a handful of other Soviet dissidents. "A creative association acting in conformity with the laws of the state," the purposes of the committee were specified as including assistance to state authorities in creating and applying safeguards for human rights, help for persons who research and study human rights in a socialist society, legal education in the field, and "constructive criticism of the present state of the Soviet system of legal safeguards for individual freedom."

Although hardly a civil libertarian organization in the Western sense of a legal interest group, the fact that the committee was openly and "legally" established and that it was seeking international support decided the league in favor of affiliation. Fears of league board members, that there would be reprisals against committee members in Moscow, were assuaged by the insistence of Russian dissidents that publicity could only strengthen their position—that silence helped no one. This, nonetheless, imposed a special responsibility upon the ILHR: to protect as well as to support the members of the Moscow Human Rights Committee.

A second experiment in strategy arises from the fact that, as the oldest international human rights NGO, the league has received an increasing number of complaints of alleged violations of human rights sent to it by individuals and organizations throughout the world—currently about one thousand such complaints annually. Since the league does not have the research (and verification) manpower and competence that Amnesty International has established with respect to political prisoners, nor does it have the legal-professional and jurisprudential prestige of the limited-membership International Commission of Jurists, the league has sought to develop its own style of response to a small sample of these unsolicited complaints.

We refer here to the Lawyers' Committee on International Human Rights, a joint effort of the International League and the Council of New York Associates (some 1,600 young "public interest" lawyers of the New York City area), established in 1976. By the end of the year it had enlisted some thirty-five young attorneys; it had held three training sessions (on international human rights law, on the United Nations and NGOs, and on new U.S. legislation on human rights); and it was generally experimenting with efforts to fulfill the felt need for "class action" intervention doctrines. The Lawyers' Committee's efforts, thus far, have been impressive.

A final form of experimentation has recently been under consideration by the league, though the board has not yet approved the strategy. This concerns the possibility of targeting league pressure on such multilateral funding agencies as the World Bank or the International Monetary Fund, on such American funding agencies as the Export-Import Bank, and perhaps even on multinational corporations, especially American multinationals. Other human rights NGOs have engaged in such action; for example, church groups and American black NGOs have tried to curtail the flow of both aid and investment to the white regimes in southern Africa by such pressure. However, when the league's board considered the transmission of a resolution to Robert McNamara, president of the World Bank—a resolution asking that the bank deny a pending loan request to Paraguay on the grounds of political repression by the military, genocide of the Ache Indians, political corruption and narcotics trafficking by or on the part of the ruling elite—this was a new departure for the league.

Traditional Strategies

Simultaneously, the league has engaged in nonexclusive and traditional strategies such as the sending of observers to political trials; the dispatch of special missions to conduct on-site investigations of selected human rights situations; and, increasingly, the staging of political-social events as political fund raisers for such extrabudgetary costs. The league has also engaged in preparing in-depth reports on priority issues and, when requested, has prepared detailed reviews of human rights violations for such congressional committees as Congressman Fraser's Subcommittee on International Organizations.

While the expertise and legitimacy of human rights NGOs like the International League or Amnesty International have given them privileged access to such committees, and to the senators and congressmen who concern themselves most with human rights, the league does not engage in lobbying within the meaning of Title III of the Legislative Reorganization Act of 1946 and subsequent federal court decisions interpreting that "Federal Regulation of Lobbying Act." That is, the league never lobbies for or against specific U.S. legislation. This notwithstanding, the league does act to shape the effective climate of political opinion in the United States and, through this indirect manner, it acts to ensure that elite behavior will be in accordance with the league's pro-human rights preferences.

Appraising Effectiveness

Any attempt to appraise both the short-term impact and the long-range effectiveness of league strategies brings one back to the issue of shadow versus substance. The league, like almost every single political interest group, lacks both the resources and the expertise to conduct objective evaluations of its own activities. Additionally, it is unable to engage in long-term planning because the human rights field is an endemic crisis situation relative to the few pro-human rights groups and their terribly limited resources. Consequently, an organization such as the league is guided by hope and faith and such crude indicators of their effectiveness as quantity and quality of press clippings about league activities.

On the other hand, the social science researcher cannot avoid the obligation of attempting an independent assessment. In this endeavor there are two extreme dangers: the first is the easy equation of activity with influence; the second is to adopt an inappropriate scientific stance—"if it cannot be counted, it does not exist"—thus denying that such groups have any intended impact. Bearing these dangers in mind, what can one conclude?

For the first twenty-five years of the league's existence, and taking its proclaimed primary function at face value, the league was highly effective. Evidence for this is found in the substantial corpus of international law on human rights drafted since World War II. However, in examining the organization's shift to its present focus—that of implementation—we have a much more complex problem of evaluation. Tentatively, the league (as one important constituent of a pro-human rights "movement") has been successful in putting human rights on the agenda of U.S. politics. Agenda setting is, of course, the classical strategy of interest groups in American politics: it makes little difference which party wins a political election so long as one can monopolize the officeholders' focus of attention.

The test, however, still lies in the future. In the Bicentennial and American presidential election year of 1976, the ILHR and other human rights NGOs were able to make human rights concerns politically salient. Yet it is by no means clear that human rights concerns can retain their high rank position in a changed environment entailing conflict with national economic goals.

Furthermore, if we expand our perspective beyond the borders of the United States, 1976 did not exhibit so nearly favorable a climate for human rights concerns. This stark fact raises a disturbing possibility: one cannot focus on the pro-human rights actors alone, isolated from the systemic context. For, if in one sense we can document heightened attention to human rights, expanded activities on behalf of human rights, in another sense the world political system may have moved toward intensified repression.

Human Rights Movement

Yet there is enough evidence of lives saved, prisoners freed, oppressors tumbled from power, to sustain the efforts of these activists. Moreover, the International League (as one of a tiny handful of human rights NGOs) has operated successfully as a catalyst of others and in ad hoc coalition building in defense of threatened rights. In the near term, while the key activists are dubious of the net gains from moving in the direction of a mass membership organization, one can expect them to build further upon the experiment with the Lawyers' Committee for International Human Rights (which would help them define a unique role) and to further cooperate in the building of a human rights movement.

Indeed, at the present time there are stirrings in Washington and New York toward the creation of a permanent coalition on human rights, which may crystallize into a form of the "Leadership Conference" which guided the successful civil rights legislation of the 1960s. The International League for Human Rights will obviously want to associate with these new strivings.□

READINGS SUGGESTED BY THE AUTHORS:

Claude, Richard P., ed. *Comparative Human Rights*. Baltimore: Johns Hopkins University Press, 1976.

Fraser, Donald M. "Freedom and Foreign Policy." *Foreign Policy*, no. 26 (Spring 1977): 140–56.

Scoble, Harry M., and Wiseberg, Laurie S. "Human Rights NGOs: Notes toward a Comparative Analysis." *Human Rights Journal* (forthcoming, 1977).

Sohn, Louis B., and Buergenthal, Thomas. *International Protection of Human Rights*. 4 vols. New York: Bobbs-Merrill, 1973.

Weissbrodt, David. "The Role of International Nongovernmental Organizations in the Implementation of Human Rights." *Texas International Law Journal* 12 (Spring/Summer 1977): 293–320.

IMPLEMENTING UNITED NATIONS COVENANTS

A.GLENN MOWER, JR.
Hanover College

U nless and until the world's governments are ready to establish a completely independent human rights organ, divorced from any semblance of governmental control, possessing independent powers in its own right, and with guarantees that its decisions will be accepted and complied with by governments, the political factor will continue to be the single most powerful determinant of the effectiveness of any international system created to protect human rights, including the one called for in the International Covenant on Civil and Political Rights. The situation remains, here as elsewhere in human affairs: the question is never *whether* there will be politics in these affairs, but whether the politics will be "good" or "bad," well managed or bungled, by people of wisdom, vision, courage, and integrity or by their opposites, responsive to human needs or oblivious to them.

Developmental Issues

The major practical problem relating to the international protection of human rights has always been the implementation of standards, and this was one of the thorniest of the issues which had to be dealt with in developing the International Covenant on Civil and Political Rights. A commitment to establish some implementary procedure was made by the UN's Commission on Human Rights (CHR) at its second session in December 1947, when it was decided that the proposed International Bill of Rights should consist of a declaration, a covenant, and measures of implementation. This was reenforced by General Assembly action in December 1948, in the form of a resolution which asked the commission to continue to give priority to the preparation of a draft covenant on human rights and draft measures of implementation.

This decision to include measures of implementation was not reached easily, for it was by no means unanimously agreed that international machinery for this purpose was either necessary, desirable, or possible. Despite these hesitations and negative attitudes, the question of international implementary machinery was settled, in principle, by the UN's Economic and Social Council (ECOSOC), which resolved on June 21, 1946 that the purpose of the United Nations with regard to the promotion and observance of human rights, as defined in the charter, could be fulfilled only if provision were made for implementation of human rights and of an international bill of rights.

The council then indicated its support for some international implementary procedures by requesting CHR to submit suggestions for effective implementation. This action also signaled the acceptance of the principle that once human rights became embodied in an international instrument, the barrier to intervention in domestic affairs no longer applied to situations covered by this instrument. Human rights, in other words, became an international matter through the existence of a covenant or convention.

Implementary Systems

In the movement toward the establishment of implementary procedures, one question which had to be answered was whether there should be one or two sets of systems—one to apply to economic, social, and cultural rights, and another to civil and political rights—or a single system to deal with both kinds of rights.

One viewpoint held that, because of the interdependence of all human rights, there were no differences between the need to ensure respect for both kinds of rights which would justify the creation of two implementary systems; the same procedure of reports by governments to ECOSOC could be used for both categories of rights. The majority opinion, however, was that there were sufficient distinctions between the two catalogs of rights to call for differing implementary approaches. The contention of these governments was that, unlike economic, social, and cultural rights, civil and political rights could be precisely defined and quickly put into effect through appropriate legislation or other governmental action; it would therefore be possible to determine, in specific cases, whether or not a violation had occurred. This being so, some implementary devices going beyond reports were possible and desirable.

Just how far beyond a report system the implementary procedure should go was, of course, the key question. A corollary problem was whether the prescribed procedure should be built into the covenant or embodied in a separate instrument. The first and most important of these two problems—the nature of the implementary system—was, in turn, seen to involve two critical issues: the organ (or organs) to be entrusted with implementation, and access to this machinery.

Implementary Organs

The question of what organ(s) should be given the responsibility for implementing the covenant produced many answers. Some of these pointed to organs already in existence: the UN Security Council, the General Assembly, and the International Court of Justice. The bulk of the discussion of implementary machinery, however, dealt with organs to be created, not those already in existence. The interest in including a judicial body in the implementary system was reflected in proposals to establish a special court of human rights.

The idea of a special court was highly controversial, as was that of creating some nonjudicial body to oversee the observance of human rights. There were also differences of opinion on the functions and powers of a supervisory organ. While there were these differences, however, there was also a mainstream of thinking about the functions of an implementary agency; this was in favor of an organ which would be a fact finder and instigator of negotiations between parties to a case arising under the proposed covenant, but not an adjudicator.

Access to Procedures

One aspect of the work of an implementary agency was particularly controversial: the source of petitions, or complaints, to be received by this agency. The question here was whether individuals and groups of individuals should be allowed to present petitions alleging violations of their rights by a government, or whether the complaint process should be restricted to states.

Those who argued for individual petition maintained that (1) a state cannot be relied upon to bring up cases arising within its own borders, and reliance on other states to take the initiative in such matters would mean that serious violations might never come to light; (2) a precedent was established for consideration of individual petitions in connection with minorities problems by the League of Nations; and (3) a fundamental basis of effective democratic government is recognition of the right of individual appeal.

Those who resisted the giving of this right of petition to individuals stressed the traditional principle of international law: that only states are subjects of international law. They also pointed to other negative features or consequences of such a grant: the possibility that this right could be used to harass and embarrass governments, and the tactical danger that, should too much stress be put on individual petition, the broader movement to produce a covenant might suffer.

The Soviet Union was opposed to *any* kind of petition procedure, whether it gave this right to states, individuals, or groups of individuals. Its argument was that the petition procedure "conflicted with the whole system of international public law regulating the relations between states," and would transform a dispute between a private individual or group of individuals and their government into an international dispute, thereby substantially enlarging the area of international differences, friction, and incidents. At the other end of the opinion pole were the French, who, in an early proposal, would have allowed the CHR to receive petitions from states, nongovernmental organizations, individuals, and groups of individuals.

The position of the United States was less clear. There was sympathy, within the government, for the idea of individual petition; but there was also a feeling that this was not, at the time, a practicable device, that it would be useful if the UN were given authority to enforce human rights and if the procedure were handled "sensibly." That the U.S. government tended toward the negative side of the question was indicated in its proposal, made jointly with the United Kingdom, limiting the complaint procedure to states. The upshot of this debate, in the early years of the UN's history, on the question of individual petition was its rejection by the CHR.

Another casualty of the early debates on implementary procedures was a rather drastic provision in the Secretariat's memorandum on implementation, calling for the establishment of local agencies of the UN in the various countries of the world, "with jurisdiction to supervise and enforce human rights therein." This was proposed as a possible "last stage" in a series of successive steps to be taken to establish a system for implementation. But given the prevailing temper of the UN's members, there was very little likelihood that any such consideration could be expected to lead to acceptance of a UN presence, within a state, with the kind of authority denoted in the Secretariat's memo.

Still another proposal for implementation which failed to win support would have created an office of a high commissioner for human rights, who would intervene in cases of violations, either ex officio or after receiving complaints. The arguments for this office were: the observance of human rights is a question of international, rather than national, interest, and as such allegations of violations, including those from individuals or groups of individuals, should be made directly to a suitable UN organ. The attorney-general (as the high commissioner was sometimes called) would represent the organization in all transactions involving the defense of human rights.

Opponents of this idea emphasized the difficulty such an official would encounter in trying to decide the truth, or falsity, of complaints. The resistance to any central UN authority endowed with meaningful supervisory powers was so prevalent through the UN membership that this proposal, too, had little chance of acceptance.

When the Draft Covenant on Civil and Political Rights reached the General Assembly for consideration, it called for implementary procedures apart from those attached to the companion covenant, on economic, social, and cultural rights. Its implementary provisions included a Committee on Human Rights which would perform fact-finding and good offices functions and opportunity for any state party to complain to the committee if it thought that another party was not meeting its covenant obligations in specific situations. These and other provisions in the Draft Covenant were placed on the agenda of the Third Committee (on Social, Humanitarian, and Cultural Matters) at its 1966 session, where much of the earlier debate on the central issues concerning implementation was repeated.

Evaluating the Machinery

What twenty years of labor produced by way of implementary machinery for civil and political rights can be summed up as "not the best, but probably the best obtainable," given the resistance of governments to any system which would be capable of exercising real power above the national level. In view of this resistance, plus the fact that until 1945 there was no international system for the protection of rights in general, the production of even a modest implementary system was a significant accomplishment.

The kind of system which was instituted with the adoption of the Covenant on Civil and Political Rights and the Protocol in 1966 was determined by the attitude with which governments approached the task of building on the charter's commitment to human rights: an attitude of wanting to do something, but not so much as to risk the loss of control over their internal affairs, or to create the means by which unfriendly governments could embarrass or harm them.

It was this attitude which created a situation where governments were made accountable to the UN for their behavior under the covenant, through a system of reports, but were given only the broadest of directions concerning what was to go in the reports. It was this attitude which permitted new ground to be broken through the creation of a special, single UN agency to provide some leadership and supervision in this field, but would not allow this agency to be more than a fact-finder, source of good offices, and conciliator. It was this attitude, too, which gave the individual a new standing by granting him the right to invoke an international agreement on his own behalf and against his government, through a petition to an international agency, but then put all this at the mercy of governments who were given the freedom to decide whether to allow individuals within their jurisdiction to exercise this right.

It was, in short, a state-centered system of implementation which emerged in 1966, one which put all the key decisions into the hands of states, and thereby enabled them to protect their prerogatives and sensitivities. But this was all that could be expected at the time. It is unfortunate, however, that the prevailing circumstances and attitudes were such as to deprive the implementary system of at least one element which is highly desirable in any system of implementation: an organ, or organs, capable of making judgments in specific cases. The rejection of any provision calling for the reference of a case to a court, or other body capable of reaching a decision, left the system "headless" in the sense of having no organ which could say with authority whether or not a government had, in fact, violated the covenant.

Even the possibility of getting an *opinion* on whether there had been a violation was lost when the Third Committee changed the functions of the proposed Human Rights Committee, as set forth in the commission's draft. This draft had empowered the committee to "draw up a report on the facts [of a case which defied friendly solution] and state its opinion as to whether the facts disclosed a breach, by the State concerned, of its obligations under the Covenant." This committee function, however, was lost in the process of creating a different kind of committee, one whose main role was to conciliate.

Conciliation is a most commendable and necessary part of the implementary process. But it must be remembered that an implementary system, to be complete, must be equipped to deal with two types of governments: those who respect human rights and want to see them enjoyed to the full, and those who have little or no regard for them. Very few governments, of course, fall completely into either of these two categories; most of them are likely to have moments when the conciliatory approach is appropriate, and moments when their attitude is too negative to permit this approach to work. Implementary systems, in other words, must be so set up and operated that the approach to governments can be on either an adversary or cooperative basis, depending on the circumstances of each case. What we have, though, is a system which must rely on only one tactic: conciliation.

Operators' Effectiveness

The effectiveness of an implementary system depends on two things: the machinery set up for this task, and the way this machinery is used, or permitted to be used. The kind of agencies created, and the functions and powers allotted to them, set limits on what can be done to give effect, on the international level, to human rights. But, within these limits, what is actually done depends on the skill and attitudes of those who operate the machinery. The kind of cautious aggressiveness of the Council of Europe's agencies and personnel has had much to do with the success of a system which provided the basic, necessary channels for both the coercive and cooperative approaches to governments; and the mainly responsive attitude of governments has had much to do, also, with this success. While the UN's system, under the covenant, is not as far-reaching and complete as is that of the Council of Europe, it can produce good results if, as in the case of the council's program, the people who manage it bring both realism and boldness to their task and governments are reasonably cooperative.

This factor raises the question of the personnel of the Human Rights Committee, a key element in the covenant's system. While this committee starts its work with a severely limited grant of authority, it does seem to have one advantage: a membership which appears to conform to the covenant's stipulation that persons elected to it should possess "recognized competence in the field of human rights." The covenant also directs that, in the selection of these people, consideration should be given to the "usefulness of the participation of some persons with legal experience."

When, in compliance with the covenant's provision, the 38 parties to the covenant met in September 1976 to elect the committee, they had 26 names from 23 states from which to choose the 18-member committee. Sixteen members were selected on the first ballot, and the remainder on the second. Of the 18, 16 could be considered as satisfying the criterion of competence in the human rights field, through either participation in various human rights enterprises or contributing to the literature in this field. Twelve of these, in turn, have legal backgrounds. Chosen to serve in their personal capacity, these committee members are distributed among five geographical/political groupings. The committee profile roughly follows that of the states party to the covenant.

Any attempt to anticipate the committee's behavior on the basis of the political background of its members is hazardous. It will be some time before the committee is tested in this regard through state-versus-state complaints, since as of September 1976 only six states had accepted this option, four short of the number required for it to be operational. The rate of progress in ratifications and acceptances also indicated that relatively few committee members would find themselves under any particular pressure to safeguard a national interest, for only seven of the eighteen come from states party to the protocol, and only four from countries accepting the states-versus-state complaint option.

Politics-Human Rights Linkage

One of the most prominent nonstructural factors likely to affect the covenant's implementary system is the one which is said to permeate all of the UN's efforts on behalf of human rights: politics. Not only does the political element exist, but it is said to weaken the organization's effectiveness in human rights questions and hamper its procedures. It is governments who determine what the UN does or does not do, and governments, in turn, are guided by political considerations which, it is argued, place limits on what governments will want done in regard to human rights situations in other areas. Thus a government will react to such a situation not on the basis of what it thinks of this situation, but according to its calculation as to whether its interests will be well served by "making a fuss" about it.

However, even if the political factor does exist, it may be viewed as a necessary and desirable part of the UN's human rights processes. Thus, it is said, given the still relatively primitive nature of the world's political society in the sense of being centered on the independent nation-state, political considerations may be the force most likely to move governments to take any action in support of human rights, or in opposition to serious departures from human rights standards. Since governments tend to act only if and when there is a national interest in so doing or some political goal to be reached, political factors and pressures are the only real leverage available either to get governments to act against unsavory human rights situations or to move a guilty government to respond affirmatively to protests against its behavior. While this approach may not appeal to one's higher sensitivities, a realist may wonder what difference it makes, whether a government moves or responds according to political motivation, as long as something gets done to enable people to enjoy their rights more completely.

At any rate, it could be argued that the whole question of the desirability or undesirability of the political factor in human rights matters is irrelevant, that politics and human rights are so interwoven that they cannot possibly be separated. According to this view, human rights are one aspect of the political process, a political tool to promote political interests; to proceed on this basis is the only "natural" way to act, since we are dealing with practical, not ideal, situations. Moreover, the discussion and disposition of human rights questions goes on within a UN which is itself a highly politicized institution.

The inevitability of the politics-human rights link is also a result of the fact that the political process involves the setting of priorities and the effort to achieve the purposes which rank high in the resulting scale. All of this is revealed in the handling of human rights on the international level. Thus a government may be accused of indifference to rights when it is really more concerned with another category of rights. A preference such as this may surface in the way a government responds to items on a human rights organ's agenda, a natural extension of the political process of priority setting to the international plane. Much of the history of the UN's struggle with human rights could be written in terms of the disagreement between East and West as to which type of national social-political organization is more oppressive of rights and, more recently, in terms of the same kind of conflict between North and South.

Responses to UN Action

One final note on the inevitability of politics within the UN's human rights process concerns this process itself. Politics is the art of the possible, and the UN's human rights organs need to be aware of what realistically can be done concerning certain situations. This becomes a matter of adopting a relativist, not absolutist, approach to human rights questions, a matter of inquiring into specific situations and reacting to them as such, not on any absolute, fixed basis of norms and expectations. It becomes, too, a matter of determining the probable response of a government to UN initiatives and shaping them accordingly.

All of these considerations raised in relation to the UN's human rights proceedings are relevant to the question of the future of the covenant's implementary system, for it too will operate in the total world environment which has surrounded the UN's efforts to date. □

READINGS SUGGESTED BY THE AUTHOR:

Carey, John B. *UN Protection of Civil and Political Rights*. Syracuse, N.Y.: Syracuse University Press, 1970.

Haas, Ernst B. *Human Rights and International Action*. Stanford, Calif.: Stanford University Press, 1970.

Korey, William. "The Key to Human Rights: Implementation." In *International Conciliation*, compiled by the Carnegie Endowment for International Peace (no. 570). New York: Carnegie Endowment for International Peace, 1968.

Robertson, A.H. *Human Rights in the World*. Manchester, England: Manchester University Press, 1972.

Van Dyke, Vernon. *Human Rights, the United States, and the World Community*. New York: Oxford University Press, 1970.

FINAL ACTS AND FINAL SOLUTIONS

WILLIAM KOREY
Human Rights Committee of the
Conference of Nongovernmental
Organization Representatives

E arly in 1977 an appeal of desperation from Soviet Jewish "refuseniks" was addressed to the chief of state of each government which approved the Helsinki "Final Act." With more signatories than any other Soviet Jewish appeal in several years—163 signers from 13 cities—the appeal emphasized that the "situation in which would-be emigrants are brought to utter despair by being constanly refused—quite illegally—for many years, can no longer be tolerated."

What the cry of Jewish despair signified was an extraordinary faith in the Helsinki Final Act, that somehow this document will finally bring redress, if not salvation, from an intolerable burden. The Jewish "refuseniks" are not alone in their faith. The many dissenters throughout Eastern Europe who long for "freer movement of peoples and ideas"—a major purpose of the Final Act—subscribe to the same hope.

Offer of Hope

Such hope did not initially prevail when the Final Act was signed on August 1, 1975 by the thirty-five countries of Europe and North America. Indeed, many of the activists and dissenters saw the document as merely one of ratifying the Yalta territorial arrangements in Eastern Europe and, therefore, Soviet domination of the area. They believed that the West had capitulated and had not extracted a genuine compensatory benefit. Andrei Sinyavsky related that he wept when he read the Helsinki accord, and he was by no means alone in the emotion.

Later Sinyavsky changed his mind. After reexamination of the document, he concluded that it offers a beacon of hope to all struggling for human rights. In fact, the Final Act has kindled aspirations and sparked demands for both emigration and greater freedom of expression. Sinyavsky warned, however, that this potential is realizeable only if the West vigorously presses on its provisions.

The potential, in fact, was present from the beginning. The Final Act of the Helsinki Conference on Security and Cooperation—to give it its formal name—which was a product of two years of laborious effort, indeed, constituted an important breakthrough with respect to human rights. For the first time in history, human rights were accorded the status of a fundamental principle in regulating interstate relations. The Final Act recognized ten fundamental principles, among which was Principle VII: "Respect for human rights and fundamental freedoms, including the freedom of thought, conscience, religion or belief." The thirty-five signatories formally declared "their intention to conduct their relations with all other states in the spirit of the principles contained in the present Declaration."

Human Rights Principle

The human rights principle, which represented the Western "quid" for the Soviet "quo" on security, is specified in concrete terms in the so-called "Basket III" of the declaration entitled "Cooperation in Humanitarian and Other Fields." Basket III embraces four sections: "Human Contacts," "Information," "Cooperation and Exchanges in the Field of Culture" and "Cooperation and Exchanges in the Field of Education." Incorporated in Basket III are the basic aspirations of Soviet Jewry: reunification of families and cultural and religious rights of minorities.

The section on human contacts has a direct relevance to the first aspiration. The participating states formally declared as "their aim to facilitate freer movement . . . and to contribute to the solution of the humanitarian problems that arise in that connection." The right of emigration is stressed here for two apparent reasons. In the first place, throughout history—from Socrates through the Magna Carta to the Universal Declaration of Human Rights—this right has been regarded as central to human liberty. In the second place, as the classic UN study by José Ingles in 1963 has demonstrated, the right to leave a country is "an indispensable condition for the full enjoyment by all of other civil, political, economic, social and cultural rights," and its deprivation "may be tantamount to the total deprivation of liberty if not life itself."

The key subsection under "Human Contacts" is specified as "Reunification of Families." It contains the following detailed obligations from the signatories: (1) they are to "deal in a positive and humanitarian spirit with persons who wish to be reunited with members of their family''; (2) applications for exit visas are to be dealt with ''as expeditiously as possible''; (3) the signatories are ''to ensure'' that the fees charged in connection with exit visas ''are at a moderate level'' and are to ''lower them when necessary''; and (4) the signatories are to treat exit visa applications in such a way that they do ''not modify the rights and obligations'' of the applicant or of members of his family.

The section on travel for personal and professional reasons calls upon the signatories to allow institutions and organizations of a religious faith to ''have contacts and meetings among themselves and exchange information.'' Principle VII of the declaration further stipulates that the signatories are to ''recognize and respect the freedom of the individual to profess and practise, alone or in community with others, religion or belief in accordance with the dictates of his own conscience.''

The provisions of the Final Act or declaration have considerable moral force in and unto themselves, even though the document is not formally a treaty and, therefore, is not necessarily binding upon the signatories. What reinforces the Final Act are its specific references to international treaties which *are* binding upon contracting parties. Principle VII specifies that the signatories of the Helsinki Final Act ''will also fulfill their obligations as set forth in the international declaration and agreements in this field, including *inter alia* the International Covenants on Human Rights, by which they are bound.''

The most important covenant is the one covering civil and political rights, which was ratified by the USSR on October 16, 1973, and which became international law on March 23, 1976 after thirty-five governments had ratified it. Article 12 of the covenant provides that ''everyone shall be free to leave any country, including his own.'' Article 27 specified that ''minorities shall not be denied the right, in community with other members of their group, to enjoy their own culture, to profess and practise their own religion, or to use their own language.''

Agreements versus Actions

Two other international agreements to which the USSR is bound are also relevant. The International Convention on the Elimination of All Forms of Racial Discrimination, in Article 5, stipulates that ratifying powers are to assure the citizen ''the right to leave any country, including his own.'' The Soviet Union ratified this treaty on January 22, 1969. The UNESCO Convention Against Discrimination in Education, in Article 5, guarantees ''the right of members of national minorities to carry on their own educational activities, including the maintenance of schools and . . . the use or the teaching of their own language.'' The treaty was ratified by the Soviet Union on August 1, 1962.

Does the Kremlin consider itself bound by the Helsinki Final Act, including the Basket III provision? Publicly the answer is yes. Spokesmen of the USSR have repeatedly, unequivocally, and unhesitatingly stated that the regime, and all Helsinki signatories, are obligated to fulfill every part of the Final Act. *Izvestiia*, in August 1975, called Helsinki "a law of international life." At the 25th Congress of the Soviet Communist Party, in February 1976, Leonid Brezhnev declared that "the main thing now is to implement in practise all of the principles and understandings agreed upon in Helsinki." The official and authoritative spokesman of the Kremlin, Leonid Zamyatin, told a national television audience last May that the Final Act requires compliance "in absolutely all its aspects by all states."

The words of the Kremlin, however, do not conform with its actual practice. A "positive and humanitarian spirit" scarcely governs, for example, the question of reunion of families. As compared with the years 1972–73, when Jewish emigration data reached a total of 67,000, during 1975–76 the emigration figures plunged to 27,000. A fairly fixed monthly rate of 1,000 appears to prevail which strongly suggests an arbitrarily and selectively determined pattern. Clearly the Kremlin is intent upon restricting the rate of emigration. Thus there exists a gross disproportion between the number of family reunion affidavits requested by Soviet Jews from relatives in Israel and the number allowed to emigrate. The former totals more than double the latter.

Emigrating Jews

Discouragement begins at the initial stage of receiving an affidavit (*vyzov*) from one's family in Israel. Would-be emigrants find that their mail is tampered with. Family members in Israel often are required to send as many as five to seven separate affidavits before one succeeds in reaching its destination. In one instance the minister of communications of the USSR told a persistent applicant of Kiev that his *vyzov* "had been lost somewhere on the territory of the USSR." In various cases Soviet officials (OVIR) refuse to recognize an affidavit unless it comes from relatives "whom you have met personally." In an agricultural region (Voronezh), where 90 out of 130 families are awaiting affidavits, the chairman of the Village Soviet, who has intercepted their mail (and in some cases has shown them to insistent Jews), told the would-be recipients, "And don't hope to get them; there's no reason for you to go to Israel."

Upon receiving the affidavits, Soviet Jews—in a number of areas—have difficulties in presenting them to local officials. In Odessa, Dushanbe (Tadzhikstan), and several other places, the OVIR offices are deliberately kept open only one or two hours a week. As a result, extremely long lines are formed to submit the documents. Many have waited as much as seven or eight months before being able to submit their affidavits.

Elsewhere, most notably in Ukrainian towns, including Kiev and Odessa, the authorities have refused to accept applications from Jews of any age whose parents do not apply to emigrate with them (even if the parents are old and very much desire their progeny to leave). Very recently an additional obstacle has been introduced. The head of the national OVIR office arbitrarily ruled that a family consists only of husband, wife, and their unmarried children. Thus he has instructed rejection of affidavits that come from older parents living in Israel, or uncles, aunts, brothers, sisters, and cousins. In making the announcement, the top OVIR official declared, "We are now putting a stop to all arbitrary emigration."

When the affidavit is received and is submitted, the torment only then begins. All sorts of capricious reasons are used in order to refuse an exit visa. Frequently the reason is the refusal of a parent, even if the applicant is a fully mature person. (At times, the parent is himself or herself intimidated, consciously or unconsciously.) A second, often repeated reason is the allegation that the applicant knows "state secrets" or was exposed to such "secrets." But in most cases of such refusals, the applicant, in fact, either never had access to "state secrets" or had ceased his employment in a security-type Soviet institution long before he made application to leave. At times the applicant is refused on grounds that his relatives who would remain in the USSR have knowledge of "state secrets." At other times he is refused because his field of research could in the future become a "state secret."

Especially arbitrary is another very frequently given reason— "considerations of regime." This vague formulation keeps the applicant totally in the dark as to what burden he is required to shed before he can receive approval from the authorities. Mystification becomes complete when another applicant with exactly the same experiences and job is granted an exit visa while he is not. Not unusual is yet another reason which provides a supreme example of caprice. The applicant is simply informed that his application is rejected because it is "inadvisable."

The "refuseniks," numbering some one thousand families who have been persistently refused exit visas, live in a state of suspended animation facing intense social ostracism. Their condition is a clear-cut breach of the obligation assumed by the USSR to deal with the applications for exit visas as "expeditiously as possible." Some "refuseniks" have waited for exit visas for as long as eight years, their repeated requests for reconsideration perenially rejected. In their appeal to the signers of Helsinki, they demanded the setting of a "time limit" for refusals.

Modifying Emigrés' Rights

Of far greater significance than the failure to treat applications in a "positive and humanitarian spirit" and as "expeditiously as possible" is the gross abridgement of the obligation to "not modify the rights" of the applicant or "members of his family." It is precisely the modification of such right through various forms of harassment and intimidation that would-be applicants are forcefully discouraged from making application for exit visas. There are seven principal forms of harassment which constitute modification of rights.

In innumerable instances applicants or sons of applicants have been suddenly drafted into the military. Previously these persons have been exempted from military service on grounds of health, age, or attendance at universities. Such exemptions are arbitrarily terminated. Estimates suggest that as many as 30 percent of all families wishing to emigrate face the threat of army conscription for themselves or for their children. Once in the military, the draftees can be charged with exposure to "state secrets" and, thereby, the possibility of even their future emigration is seriously jeopardized.

An applicant who attends university or the progeny (of an applicant) who is attending university is frequently deprived of rights through expulsion from the university or an institution of higher learning. They are advised that the application for emigration is behavior not befitting a Soviet citizen.

Upon application for an exit visa, the applicant is either demoted or more often fired from his job. This deprives him of his livelihood which is further aggravated if a long delay ensues in granting him an exit visa. He may be and often is threatened with the legal charge of "social parasitism," even though employers are reluctant to or refuse to employ his skills. The device has all the earmarks of "Catch 22." In March 1977 one of the leading activists, Iosif Begun, was convicted of "parasitism" and sentenced to a two-year period of exile.

Scientists and technically trained persons who have applied for exit visas are prevented from participating in academic conferences and seminars, sometimes of the most informal kind. In this way their skills and knowledge are deleteriously affected and their potential for future employment is seriously reduced.

In certain areas of the USSR applicants for exit visas must immediately give up their apartments even before their application is considered, let alone granted. Thus they are deprived of the basic shelter to permit survival.

Those who are obliged to wait for long periods after making application for an exit visa have been dependent on material assistance sent on a humanitarian basis by well-wishers from abroad. Until 1976 such assistance had been seriously reduced by a 30 percent "bank-handling" surcharge imposed on these gifts. In January 1976 the problem was profoundly aggravated by an additional 35 percent surcharge and by restrictions upon the value and size of parcels sent to the recipient. The assessed value of a parcel has, in consequence, been raised to as much as eight to ten times its normal value. A veritable confiscatory tax has, thereby, been arbitrarily imposed.

In various instances applicants for exit visas have been threatened with arrests. They can recall the trials and sentences in previous years imposed upon those seeking to emigrate. Some twenty "prisoners of conscience" are currently detained in Soviet prisons or labor camps for seeking to exercise their right to leave a country. In January 1977 the authorities moved from mere threats to actual arrests with the incarceration of a Jew from Uzbekistan, A. Zavurov, who sought to emigrate. Later, on March 15, Anatoly Shcharansky was arrested and charged with treason, in a case reminiscent of the infamous "Doctors' Plot."

Nor does an enlightened policy prevail with respect to "moderate" fees for emigration purposes. The USSR requires, since January 1976, an exit visa fee of 300 rubles per person. This hardly "moderate" figure amounts to two to three months' earnings of an average Soviet citizen. Moreover, the applicant is compelled to pay an additional 500 rubles for purposes of renouncing his Soviet citizenship. The total of 800 rubles is extremely burdensome. For a family of four persons the cost of emigration is approximately equal to three years' salary for a secretary, and a half-year's salary for a university professor.

Cultural Rights

Noncompliance with the Helsinki accord in the area of "reunion of families" also applies to the question of cultural rights. A distinguishing feature of the Soviet Jewish community since 1948 and a feature which makes its plight so poignant is the absence of national or ethnic institutions. Not a single Jewish school or even a single Jewish class exists anywhere in the USSR; not a single cultural, artistic, or publication establishment; not a single communal establishment. Such deprivation contrasts sharply with virtually every other national or ethnic group in Soviet society. And the deprivation stands in glaring contradiction to Soviet law and ideology as well as to the Kremlin's international treaty obligations, such as the International Convenant on Civil and Political Rights and the UNESCO Convention Against Discrimination in Education.

The specific obligation undertaken by the USSR under the Helsinki Declaration to recognize the contribution of national minorities and "to facilitate this contribution" is observed in the breach so far as the Soviet Jewish community is concerned. Not only has no effort been made since August 1, 1975 to restore the national, linguistic, and cultural rights of Jews; where Soviet Jews, on their own, have undertaken a determined initiative to create Jewish cultural mechanisms, they have met with resistance and repression by the authorities.

Thus a relentless campaign has been conducted by the authorities against the cultural and nonpolitical and self-produced journal, *Jews in the USSR*. Over one hundred Jews have been interrogated by police officials with the obvious intention of harassing persons who conceivably might be associated with its production. Thus, too, in July-August 1975 proceedings were undertaken against leaders of Jewish cultural seminars and Hebrew-teaching groups. In September-October similar hostile official acts were launched against the editors of the Jewish cultural review—*TARBUT*. During November-December numerous others associated with Jewish cultural activity were subjected to various forms of intimidation, including house searches and preventive arrests.

The climax of the campaign against Jewish culture came in December 1976. A scheduled seminar on December 21–23 in which some fifty scholarly papers were to be read was brutally suppressed, the papers confiscated, and the organizers of the seminar arrested. Even Jewish national-cultural programs from outside the USSR face suppression. Radio broadcasts from Israel which carry such programs are heavily jammed.

Religious Persecution

Another attribute to Soviet Jewry's plight is to be found in the area of religion (as distinct from culture and ethnic communality). Judaism in the USSR is plagued by disabilities that do not obtain for other major recognized religions. No central or federative institutional structure exists for Judaism in contrast to that which prevails for the other recognized religions; no formal association or contacts with international (or regional) rabbinic or congregational bodies are permitted. No Hebrew Bible has been published since 1929, and only on two occasions since the forties have a relatively small and inadequate number of prayer books been published. Judaism is not allowed to produce religious devotional articles such as prayer shawls and phylacteries.

Only one Yeshiva (similar to a seminary) exists in the USSR, and it does not have a single student studying for the rabbinate. The number of synagogues in the USSR has been reduced to sixty-one, and the number of rabbis is inconsequential—possibly one-half dozen. In sum, formal Judaism in the USSR is poised upon an abyss of veritable nonexistence.

While the Helsinki Declaration requires the recognition of religious freedom and specifically allows for "contacts and meetings" to "exchange information," Soviet authorities have done nothing since August 1, 1975 to provide the essentials for freely observing the Judaic faith. Indeed, specific "contacts and meetings" among Jewish observers are discouraged through random police action against assemblages of Jews who gather in front of the Moscow synagogue. Such occurrences have taken place on the Sabbath and on such holidays as Passover. Nor are "contacts" encouraged with transnational Jewish bodies. Even a primary form of communication, the telephone, has been severed for many of those Jews who are actively seeking to emigrate.

At the same time, Soviet official propagandists, through books, journals, newspapers, and lectures, have been conducting a ferocious and virulent campaign against Judaism and its principal works—the Torah and the Talmud. The campaign, which is directly linked with a propaganda drive against Zionism, gives expression to insidious forms of anti-Semitism. Such propaganda subverts the very purpose and intent of the Helsinki Declaration.

Implementing the Final Act

At Helsinki President Gerald Ford declared that "history will judge this Conference not by what we say today, but what we do tomorrow—not by the promises we make, but by the promises we keep." How to compel the signatories to keep their "promises" is thus the critical issue. President Jimmy

Carter observed that "consummation of the Helsinki agreement concerning human rights would be an ever-present consideration" in his thinking about Soviet-American relations. That human rights, indeed, constitute "a central concern" of the Carter administration has been made patently clear in the president's letter of February 5, 1977 to Andrei Sakharov, in the State Department's denunciation of the Czech repression of the "Charter 77" signers, in Secretary of State Cyrus Vance's testimony to a Senate committee on February 24, 1977, and in various comments by President Carter at press conferences.

The issue becomes how to translate the "central concern" for human rights into the formulation of precise strategies for giving effect to the Helsinki Final Act. Extensive documentation of noncompliance by the Kremlin has been accumulated by Congressman Dante Fascell's fifteen-member Commission on Security and Cooperation. When and how to use the documentation is crucial; so is the question of assuring means for periodic assessment of Helsinki's obligations. Only in this way can the Final Act take on meaning. Only then can the cry of the Moscow Jewish activists find an echo.□

READINGS SUGGESTED BY THE AUTHOR:

Basket III: Implementation of the Helsinki Accords. Hearings before the Commission on Security and Cooperation in Europe. Volumes II and III. Washington, D.C.: Government Printing Office, 1977.

Conference on Security and Cooperation in Europe. Final Act. Command. 6198, H.M. Stationary Office, London, 1975.

Korey, William. "Preparing for the Helsinki Assignment." *The New Leader*, 11 April 1977, pp. 8–9.

Roth, Stephen, J. "Facing the Belgrade Meeting." *Soviet Jewish Affairs* 7, no. 1 (1977): 1–16.

U.S., Department of State, Special Report. "Second Semi-Annual Report to the Commission on Security and Cooperation in Europe, December 1, 1976—June 1, 1977." Report No. 34, June 1977.

HUMAN RIGHTS AND WORLD RESOURCES

A. BELDEN FIELDS
University of Illinois at Urbana

This essay is divided into two parts. The first part is devoted to the presentation of data. Here the distribution of income and wealth within the capitalist
industrialized societies, as well as the share of the world GNP which is located
within these societies, is examined. The second part contains an evaluation and
a recommendation. It raises the ethical question of whether the described
situation should bother our consciences. Concluding that it should, it offers a
policy recommendation for the achievement of greater distributional equity.

Economic Inequality: Cross-National Comparisons

The data which are most often referred to in discussing ranges of inequality
are wages and salaries, sometimes loosely referred to as income. These data
must be used cautiously because wages and salaries are obviously not the only
form of income. People can be "paid" in a number of ways and from a number
of sources, some of which are reported on tax forms and accounting ledgers and
some of which are not. Entrepreneurs receive profits, stockholders receive
dividends, savings account depositers and bondholders receive interest, executives are often paid in stock options and services such as company cars,
government and party officials receive similar services and sometimes money
under the counter, heirs inherit wealth, and people profit from speculation in
property, securities, and other commodities. None of this can really be called
wages or salaries, and if it is not reported on tax returns it is not even called

126

income. Thus by focusing on wages and salaries we are in fact eliminating most of the very wealthy who are not salaried but who rely upon the above forms of income. Whatever income inequality can be discovered through examination of wage and salary statistics represents only a small part of the total inequality of wealth holding and living conditions which actually exists within any society.

It should also be kept in mind that welfare payments and services can have an equalizing effect, but only if they are maintained at a sufficiently high level and only if they truly involve transfers from the higher- to the lower-income strata. This, of course, involves the system of taxation. If the people on the bottom of the ladder pay for their own services because of regressive taxation, such payments and services are obviously not equalizers.

Comparative income data reveal important differences in the relative rankings of most of the capitalist countries—but not of France. According to the criteria used in data collection, France comes out on the low end of the equality spectrum among capitalist industrialized countries. There is a considerable spread between France, one of the least equalitarian capitalist industrialized countries, and the United States, whose equalitarian ranking is near the middle.

It is at least theoretically possible that some of the income inequality reflected in wage data could be compensated for by social welfare services and payments. What evidence is available, however, points to a minimal equalitarian impact, if any, of welfare payments in the capitalist industrialized societies. One of the earliest writers to raise the question on a comparative basis was Margaret Gordon. Gordon examined data on social security programs in thirty countries on all of the continents. In terms of the degree to which such programs are equalitarian, Gordon summarizes:

> To the extent that vertical income redistribution occurs as a result of welfare programs, it tends to be largely from average workers to families whose capacity to participate in the labor force is, for some reason, impaired. Or, as it has sometimes been put, most of it occurs within the income group under about $5,000. In countries with extensive family allowance systems, transfers from small to large families are also of considerable significance.

Writing in 1971, eight years after Gordon, Robert J. Lampman points out that up to 1967, public welfare programs since World War II have not modified the aggregate income stratification pattern of families in the United States. In an address given in October 1976, Lampman noted that when the family share of income in the United States is divided by fifths, there appears to have been no change in the stratification since 1960. He came to the conclusion that the pattern of inequality in the United States seemed to be fixed, although he noted shifts in the relative constituency of the worst off. He noted an increase in black income as a percentage of white but a deterioration of the relative position of women's wages as a percentage of men's. Single people living as family units also seemed relatively more deprived. But the structure of inequality has persisted for the past decade and a half, and Lampman estimated the present poverty income gap in the United States at $12 billion. Others have noted the same phenomenon. Further, even if the goal of welfare programs is income maintenance at a minimum level of ability to consume the array of goods produced rather than equalization, it is not terribly effective at achieving that goal.

But even with these facts, we do not get a full picture of economic inequality. When we look at the total distribution of personal wealth rather than just income, we find that the disparities are much greater. Lester Thurow has reported that while the top one-fifth of all American families receive 43 percent of what the Census Bureau considers income, that same top fifth possesses almost 80 percent of the total national wealth. While there is some variation in income inequality among the capitalist industrialized countries and considerable variation in the delivery of social services, none of them seem to have made great strides in income equalization. A 1976 report on income distribution issued by the Organization for Economic Cooperation and Development reveals very little change in the relative shares of the 20 percent of the population worst off and the 20 percent best off in the United States and the German Federal Republic, and some small advance in an equalitarian direction in France over the past fifteen years. But the advance has been so small that of the countries ranked, France still came out the most inequalitarian.

Worldwide Inequality

If the degree of inequality within capitalist industrialized countries is viewed as high, the worldwide spread of inequality is even greater. Angelos Angelopoulos cites inequalities within Third World societies: in Latin America 5 percent of the population takes 31.5 percent of the aggregate GDP (aggregate production of goods and services); 10 percent of the Latin American population takes 40–45 percent of the GNP; in ten African countries 5 percent of the population receives 40–50 percent of the GDP; in India in 1960, 10 percent of the population took 36 percent of the GDP.

Moreover, a study of forty-three "developing" countries by Irma Adelman and Cynthia Taft Morris shows that only among some of the most highly developed countries in the sample (Argentina, Chile, Taiwan, and Israel) is the income distribution as equal as it is among countries which have undergone almost no development, such as Dahomey, Chad, and Niger. Below the level of the very top layer in the sample, there is a negative relationship between economic development and equality of distribution. Furthermore, the average income of the very poor in these societies declines in absolute as well as relative terms as one ascends the levels of development.

In the absence of long-term time series or longitudinal data, the study deduces the impact of longer-term economic change from cross-sectional data. While the data suggest that the relationship over time might be U-shaped, that is, greater equality of distribution of income at the least developed and most highly developed of the Third World stages, between the two stages there is the likelihood of a double process of increased inequality and absolute immiserization of those on the very bottom for a considerable time.

As Johan Galtung has never tired of point out, the most striking disparities in the modern world are between those who own large shares of wealth within the capitalist industrialized societies as well as some of those with whom they directly conduct business in the Third World, and the masses of people in the Third World. Modern technology and the internationalization of private investment and business has created large amounts of wealth since World War II. Within the capitalist industrialized societies this has not been accompanied by equalization in the possession of wealth. It has been accompanied by welfare policies with limited distributive impact, as well as by wage levels well above the prewar levels. There is, however, considerable variation in these levels by country and by category of workers (skill level and unionization). Both inequality and poverty persist within the industrialized countries.

But as world productivity has increased, even greater disparities have developed between the top wealth holders in both the capitalist industrialized and the Third World countries and the mass of the Third World people, without the mitigation of welfare policies and labor union pressures in favor of the latter. The international system of stratification portrayed by Lenin, with admitted increases in the absolute levels of well-being among certain categories of workers in the capitalist industrialized countries, is still a highly accurate description of the distribution of wealth within the nonsocialist world, where approximately 77 percent of the total world GNP and 67 percent of the world population resided in 1970.

Moral Problem and Policy Implications

Should we be bothered by this situation? If so, what are the political or policy implications?

There is the argument that without weighing any other social values, equalization itself is unjust in either a natural or a conventional sense. The argument that equalization involves a natural injustice is based upon the premise that there are natural distinctions among people and that these distinctions merit economic differentiation. The earliest full political tract in the known history of Western philosophy, Plato's *Republic*, accepted natural distinctions. Plato's student, Aristotle, also accepted natural distinctions among people. In the eighteenth century Edmund Burke cited scripture to prove that attempts to equalize were unnatural, but the real thrust of his argument was conventional. Even Rousseau, perhaps the greatest advocate of equality in the eighteenth century, was bothered by the ex post facto problem involved in the expropriation of property which was acquired under a system where it was legally sanctioned. The dictates of natural and conventional justice began to conflict.

There are the arguments which do not claim that inequality is just in either a natural or a conventional sense, but that the pursuit of the value of equality must, or is likely to, conflict with other values. Certainly one of the most often cited values placed in jeopardy, from Toqueville to Goldwater and Friedman, is liberty. While Rousseau claimed that civil liberty was impossible without a high degree of economic equality, there are at least four arguments to the contrary. The first, the classical political economist position enunciated by John Locke, is that there can be no freedom without economic freedom. The second fears that redistribution to X extent within Y time period would necessitate the creation of oppressive political structures, that is, political parties and bureaucracies which would monopolize political power (thus instituting another kind of inequality) in order to pursue their goal of economic equalization in the face of opposition. The third major argument fears the damaging impact of attempts at equalization on competition and, therefore, productivity. Finally, the fourth argues that equalization will diminish what is commonly referred to as the "quality of life."

There is also the argument which declares the fruitlessness of equalization projects. This is to say that given the population in society X, redistribution from the wealthier to the poorer categories would be more a punishment for the wealthy than of any substantial benefit to the poor. If we look at the situation from a global perspective, the futility appears even greater. What would be the total net result if all of the personal wealth in the industrialized and nonindustrialized world were pooled and divided evenly on a per capita basis? Some would argue that there would be a minimal increase in the share of the very poorest and a disasterous decrease in productivity among the industrialized countries because of disincentive. They would argue that we would reverse the utilitarian formula by generalizing misery rather than confining it.

Plato, Rousseau, Burke

The argument that income or wealth equalization would involve either a violation or conformity with natural justice must rest essentially on two bases—the natural similarities and dissimilarities among human beings and the relevance of economic differentiation or equalization to such similarities or dissimilarities.

While the thrust of Plato's argument in the *Republic* involves differentiation according to intelligence, there is also an admission of similarity. This is in the concept of "natural need." Plato attempts to strip his ruling class of all possessions that do not conform to the requisites of natural need. They will share food, clothing, shelter, and sexual partners. Moreover, they will have a "community," a set of interrelationships which would meet the nonphysical natural needs.

What Rousseau perceived in Plato's writing was an unfair trade-off. The people of lesser intelligence could have most of the money and material goods in the state. In return they would provide for the natural physical needs of the intelligent rulers. However, they give up something much more. They also give up all power of decision making over their lives. Just as in Hobbes, where we know almost nothing about the actual lives of those living under the sovereign, we know virtually nothing of the lives of the people of lesser intelligence in Plato's *Republic*. Rousseau perceives this deprivation of basic human needs in both Plato and Hobbes. The important point is that Rousseau, in response to the classical emphasis upon difference in capability or virtue, stressed similarity of need and moral capacity. Rousseau's concept of need included both physical or psychological needs and social and community needs.

The conventional argument as put forward by Burke is difficult to answer theoretically because an important component of it is the rejection of theory in the sense of having recourse to universal arguments which transcend the specific society under consideration. However, since it is a theory itself, or at least an interpretation of how society "works" and an acceptance of how society "works" in both a positive and moral sense, it involves a certain paradox—and one which is very useful to its proponents. The only criterion which seems to emerge from Burke's thinking is a quantitative one—incrementalism. Historically change does take place, but the smaller the change over the longer time period, the better. Burke is similar to Hegel in that the "is" and the "ought" merge into one at any particular point in history.

The key to the imperative for equalization lies in Rousseau's and Abraham Maslow's concept of human needs. Our most basic physical needs—food, clothing, shelter, medical care, and so on—can only be met by commodities, property, or services which have monetary value in most societies. Our safety needs are highly contingent upon the protection which we can count on from the enforcement agencies in our societies and from the treatment which we can expect from the judicial system. Both of these are correlative with wealth and with the status which wealth brings. Self-actualization within any cultural context is dependent upon access to educational structures and to the variety of occupational roles available within the society. Again, these are correlative with income and wealth.

Finally, wealth is also a, if not *the*, major political resource. Rousseau contends that those who possess disproportionate wealth will also inevitably possess disproportionate political power over others. This will involve the triumph of particular interest and the destruction of the community, a serious deprivation of the belongingness need even for those whose particular interests triumph. For Rousseau there can be no community, nor can anyone have any morally meaningful freedom in the inequalitarian society.

Objections to Equalization

The first objection to equalization attempts based upon value conflicts was that these attempts violated freedom or liberty. Two different arguments were made. First, there was the argument that economic freedom is basic to all other freedoms. Second, there was the argument that while the aim of equalization is not in itself offensive, the process of equalization would bring with it political structures of an oppressive nature.

One obvious problem is the different nature of the concepts. Equality, particularly if we are specifically referring to economic equality, is a measurable concept. But the concept of freedom or liberty is not so easily handled empirically. Correlations between equalizing social policies and lack of freedom are established by definition among those who accept the position that economic freedom is the basis of all other freedoms. Britain and Sweden would be seen as less "free" than the United States because there is a higher degree of income equality assured by social policies in those two countries. And that would be the end of the argument.

The second argument is more potent because it discusses a more specific structural relationship. Without sanctifying property as a natural and inalienable right, it is contended that attempts to equalize would lead to the development of political apparatuses which would aggravate the problem of political equality and threaten other civil rights—such as the right to oppose vocally the policy of equalization. The proponents of this position might point to the experience of Marxist-Leninist regimes to support their position. Whatever our own views on these regimes might be, there is still the problem of comparing degrees of freedom cross-nationally and across systems. Moreover, even if we come to the conclusion that there is a higher degree of equality of wealth and income accompanied by less freedom to dissent verbally, to move freely, and so on, we still cannot subject all proposals to equalize to an identification with these regimes without falling into the above argument by definition. There are equalitarian movements on the Left—Trotskyist, anarchist, social democratic, and Marxist humanist—which have supported measures of equalization and which have been self-conscious of the dangers of having recourse to single legitimate parties and uncontrolled bureaucratic structures to carry out the policies.

To turn the argument around, however, the libertarian proponent of equalization can point out at least two ways in which the inequalitarian distribution of wealth is a threat to freedom. First, economic structures can be coercive and limit choice just as what are usually referred to as political structures can. Second, even if we were to accept a strict separation between political and economic structures and argue that freedom or liberty pertained only to the political context, we would have to raise the question of the importance of wealth as a political resource.

Similarly, the question of the relationship between incentives and productivity is not as purely "factual" as it might appear at first. Like the problem of freedom, there is no flat answer to the incentive question because there is no mechanistic relationship between "productivity" and economic differentials in the abstract. Most of those who present the argument in favor of differentials for incentive reasons, assume the parameters of the system and value it for reasons other than total productivity, for example, immediate interest or a philosophical commitment to natural property and economic rights. On the other hand, even a country such as the USSR which has eliminated private investment (at least from its own population, if not from foreign and multinational corporations) still is making use of piecework remuneration for manual labor.

Bertrand de Jouvenal grants for the sake of argument that equalization (''redistribution'') might be accomplished without a decrease in productivity. But he raises some very serious questions about what it would do to the qualitative aspect of life. He directs his concern not to the amount produced but to the excellence of the products. Briefly put, the question is, ''Must equalization mean standardization—and at a pretty low standard at that?'' It could, but it does not need to—for three reasons:

- While systems of taxation obviously must be highly centralized and standardized, there could still be considerable variation and diversity in the provision of products and services.
- By equalizing we would be able to take advantage of the brains and talents of creative people which are now lost to us because of severe deprivation.
- If we should attempt to equalize, particularly on a worldwide scale, there might be a decrease in the variety of consumer goods as the result of the establishment of priorities for investment based upon the needs of the severely deprived.

The last argument against equalization is the ''fruitlessness'' one: that if we divided up the total wealth in a particular society or internationally on an equal per capita basis, we would generalize misery. There would not be enough to affect significantly the lives of those who were previously on the bottom, and the formerly wealthy—and perhaps the middle classes—would be made miserable. I have not attempted such calculations and I do not know if this is true. Moreover, I do not need to make such calculations because that is not what I am about to propose.

Recognizing Universal Rights and Human Dignity

What I offer as a ''minimum'' proposal consistent with the recognition of universal rights and human dignity, is that the obligation to equalize income and wealth be recognized up to the point that there is no longer a correlation between certain life chances and wealth. The equalization would take place at two levels, internationally and within national societies. The task internationally is to redistribute to the point that the physical needs of people are met at an equally high level regardless of where they live. Such variables as longevity, malnutrition, and maternal and infant mortality should be charted on a worldwide basis.

Within societies the same effort should be made to eliminate discrepancies along the above dimensions. In addition, there are other dimensions of inequality which are more culturally specific and determined than the above but which still affect the meeting of natural human needs. While Maslow's love and esteem needs have greater personal than political relevance, the safety, self-actualization, and belongingness needs have direct political relevance. The safety needs relate to the degree of protection which one can expect from law enforcement and from judicial processes; the self-actualization needs relate to educational and occupational structures. That the satisfaction of these needs must take place within culturally conditioned institutional frameworks does not make the needs any less natural, in the sense of all people having them, than the physical or physiological needs.

This proposal carries with it a certain number of corollary points. (1) It is a minimal proposal in that it advocates no quick, basic institutional change such as a political revolution in the capitalist industrialized countries. (2) It is based upon a set of values which are made explicit. (3) It treats the arguments against equalization seriously, rejecting the natural inequality argument but treating the conventional arguments with some care. (4) It is offered without claiming that income equalization is the sole consideration in social justice or the social good. (5) However, the recognition of natural needs is not the "degeneration" into a kind of quantitative utilitarianism with no, or at best a mindless, qualitative dimension. (6) A number of notions which are common in the interest group or pluralistic liberalism which dominates political science in the United States are rejected. (7) To aim at equalization presumes a certain degree of knowledge about the actual distribution of income and wealth. (8) Both income and wealth must be taxed progressively and the revenue thereby derived must be either diverted directly or converted into goods and services to meet the natural needs of those who would be so deprived without redistribution. (9) A portion of the revenue derived within the industrialized countries through internal progressive taxation should go to an international redistributive body. (10) Whether within countries or internationally, systems of taxation must be highly centralized.

Human Problem

Some might argue that this proposes too much, that "equality of opportunity" is as much as we can aim for. But how can we have "equality of opportunity" without equality in fact along those dimensions listed above? How can a child who has suffered from malnutrition compete with one who has not? How can a child who has been sorely disadvantaged educationally compete with a child who has had a superior education?

In other words, equality of opportunity is a myth without a certain minimum level of equality of result. This is perhaps why quotas are so severely rejected by many of the proponents of "equality of opportunity." It is more comfortable to bask in the myth of "equality of opportunity," fortified by that of the inevitable convergence of total productivity and equalization, than to face the fact that the problem of inequality is a human problem which must be faced by human will. Precise indicators which reflect the real-life conditions of the people on the bottom must serve as checks upon our affluent optimism that if the world is a pretty good place for us materially, it must be getting better all the time for everyone. □

READINGS SUGGESTED BY THE AUTHOR:

Annals of the American Academy of Political and Social Science, vol. 409 (September 1973): special issue devoted to the theme "Income Inequality."

de Jouvenal, Bertrand. *The Ethics of Redistribution.* Cambridge: At the University Press, 1951.

Rawls, John. *A Theory of Justice.* Cambridge, Mass.: Harvard University Press, 1971.

Rousseau, Jean-Jacques. "Discourse on the Origin of Inequality Among Men." In *The Social Contract and Discourses,* edited by G.D.H. Cole. New York: E.P. Dutton, 1950.

Thurow, Lester C. *Generating Inequality: Mechanisms of Distribution in the U.S. Economy.* New York: Basic Books, 1975.

EXAGGERATING THE COMMUNIST MENACE

TOM J. FARER
Rutgers University

From the Revolutionary War to this day, concern for human rights has been a prominent theme in the rhetoric of American foreign policy. From time to time it probably has affected the reality as well.

The decades of the Cold War were no exception. Ostensibly we opposed the spread of Soviet and Chinese power not only for amoral reasons of state, but also, as we constantly reiterated, to defend the reality and expand the possibility of human freedom. Why, then, are we flattered or agitated—as the individual case may be—by the sense of a new departure? In part, of course, because during the Kissinger years, the theme of moral conflict was consciously muted; in equal or larger part because for the first time since the end of World War II, the executive branch seems broadly willing to recognize violations of human rights in states ruled by anticommunist regimes.

The conspiracy of silence about the more nauseating participants in the "free world coalition" has collapsed. In the wake of its collapse we have witnessed some tentative steps to translate candor into effective action.

Permanent Enemies and Bad Friends

Of the varied obstacles to effective action, few are more intimidating than our visceral hostility to Third World movements whose leaders profess or at least are alleged to profess inspiration from some variant of the Marxist faith. Our determined opposition to such radical movements is reiterated in the daily gestures of the national mind.

Our fear and loathing of Marxist movements has helped propel us into indiscriminate support of right-wing regimes, including many whose behavior is characterized by persistent and gross violation of human rights. In the past proposals to disengage from the more atrocious governments, much less to punish and thus in some cases incidentally destabilize them, have often been aborted by fears that diminished U.S. support might lead to their replacement by regimes of the Left. This fear continues, albeit less openly and with somewhat less effect, to influence the debate over *means* for curbing violations of human rights. The putative Marxist threat is certain to remain a salient concern in this respect because right-wing, Third World regimes are the most susceptible to the sanctions and incentives we are able to deploy on behalf of human rights.

There has clearly been a fundamental change of perspective in the White House and the highest reaches of the State Department, a change exemplified by UN Ambassador Andrew Young who has stated unequivocally that a repressive, right-wing regime's invocation of the Marxist threat will no longer suffice to attract U.S. support. But the House of Representative's vote to bar aid to Mozambique and Angola illustrates the continued strength of the traditional mind set.

Policy Motivations

My assumption that an antiradical bias has powerfully influenced the shape of U.S. foreign policy is not wholly uncontroversial; in earlier exposures it has encountered two centers of resistance. One marshals such acts as our post-1948 entente with Marshall Tito and our brief flirtation with Kwami Nkrumah as decisive evidence of our freedom from any dogmatic antagonism to leftist regimes. The other insists that our support of rightist governments stems primarily from U.S. efforts to contain the aggressive thrust of the Soviet Union rather than from a profound ideological bias against Marxist movements, however free from Soviet domination. Both of these arguments are unpersuasive.

All the cases cited to demonstrate a shrewd, flexible discrimination are instances of pragmatic relations with *established governments*. Wherever we had a choice among competitors for power—as we did in the Belgian Congo and Angola, in Guyana and Indochina and the Dominican Republic—we sought with varying degrees of effort to block the accession of leaders who identified themselves as leftists. Moreover, where leftists formed governments but, as in Guatemala and more recently in Chile, seemed vulnerable to rightist opponents, we have been inclined to conspire with the latter to destroy the former.

Only by substituting faith for reason can we construe U.S. behavior as a purely defensive response to the hegemonic ambitions of the Soviet Union. The Russia-centered explanation of U.S. foreign policy becomes still less satisfactory when we turn to the whole counterinsurgency phenomenon. Counterinsurgency was always more than a set of tactics. It was inspired by an ideology, a world view in which apostles of open and closed economic systems, of consumer-oriented and demand economies, were locked in global combat. What was at stake, the ideologues of counterinsurgency argued, were two ways of life, two forms of political and economic development, and two visions of global order. Walt Rostow placed Vietnam in this larger context when he spoke exultantly of Ho as the last of the romantic revolutionaries. Ho Chi Minh was not a proxy for the Communist giants; rather, he was the expression of an ideology of development which it was in our interest to obstruct.

Why? That was always less clear. Different advocates had different theories. Some invoked security needs, but the reference was often circular, since prominent among the needs in question were those of the incumbents whom the theory itself assumed we had to protect. Others spoke of access to raw materials, the security of and opportunities for U.S. investors, and the availability of markets for our exports. But these latter themes, so pronounced in U.S. policy for over a half-century before World War II, were curiously muted. In the face of the Leninist claim that economic interests determine foreign policy in capitalist countries, American statesmen suddenly seemed diffident about declaring publicly the salience of such interests—hence the determined effort to force the great bulk of U.S. coercive activity under a classic, balance-of-power blanket.

Arguably inadequate as a wrap for all our policies on the periphery of China and the Soviet Union, in Latin America the security rationale seems no larger than a loin cloth, covering some vital parts but leaving others prominently exposed. It may not even cover Cuba very well, the case most frequently cited to support the proposition that revolutionary regimes have an almost irresistible impulse for military cooperation with the Soviet Union. What advocates of this proposition normally fail to note is that to a revolutionary like Castro, secretly determined on the radical transformation of his society, there were ample reasons to expect the worst from the United States once his intentions became clear.

Military Security

Given what we have learned in the sixteen years since the Green Berets marched into Vietnam, what can reasonably be said now about the security implications of a multiplication of regimes trying to adapt Chinese, Cuban, or Russian development models to their own national conditions? First, let us reaffirm the circularity of one segment of the security argument: in order to preserve right-wing governments almost everywhere, we have opposed the triumph of a radical movement almost anywhere. Thus, if we relax our rigid definition of the enemy, a significant chunk of the security problem slides away.

The other principal dimension of the problem has been governed by military requirements flowing directly from our competitive relations with the Soviet Union and China. In the Third World we have sought to acquire bases for ourselves while denying them to our adversaries. The abatement of our Chinaphobia, combined with dramatic changes in military technology, has vastly diminished our need for overseas bases. Technology has also reduced the potential benefit of such bases to the Soviet Union, except in connection with its expanded naval operations. For a number of reasons, including reliance on land-based air power and smaller service forces, base rights are in fact more important to the Russian Navy than to ours. Soviet failure to acquire base rights in Mozambique or Angola should therefore discourage any facile equation of a radical triumph in a Third World state with the promotion of Soviet security interests.

It does not follow that considerations of military security can never justify a preference for one domestic political faction over another. Where one faction is more likely to threaten a neighbor whose security remains somehow linked to our own, we should prefer and in modest ways encourage the other. And in the unlikely event of a faction genuinely determined to submit to Soviet discipline even after it acquires the rudder of state, we should again naturally prefer its opponent. But in the overwhelming majority of internal conflicts, security factors do not justify our involvement even as cheerleaders.

Economic Security

Military security has not, of course, been the exclusive justification for the powerful American bias against radical movements in the Third World. Other considerations of state have buttressed it. Economic interests may appear a little crass, slightly embarrassing; but it would be fatuous to suggest that they are negligible factors in shaping the attitudes which dominate day-to-day American diplomacy.

Wherein lies the radical threat? Are radical regimes more likely to nationalize existing American investments? Less likely to compensate adequately? Less likely to encourage new capital investment? Less open to foreign trade? And does it really matter very much? Concern over the safety of existing investment rests on the following assumptions: that radicals are more likely to expropriate U.S. holdings, less likely to pay adequate compensation, and that the resulting costs to the American people are not inconsequential. What are the facts?

Both moderate and conservative Third World governments, driven like their radical counterparts by a passion for autonomy, have themselves demonstrated a lusty appetite for national ownership of important industrial and natural resources. Nationalization of our most valuable investments, the oil concessions, proceeds in impeccably conservative as well as radical states. There is, in fact, no evident correlation between the pace and extent of nationalization in a given oil producer and the ideological bent of its rulers.

While conservative governments prove themselves susceptible to the virus of nationalization, certain left-wing governments preserve or solicit foreign investments. The pattern of compensation for nationalized investments also is rather more diverse than many American businessmen probably imagine. It is unclear, however, how much freight these precedents will carry. Furthermore, perhaps more important than the peculiarities of each case are the environments in which they arise, an environment usually characterized by American hostility to radicals and a tradition of U.S. intervention often encouraged and sometimes facilitated by U.S. corporations.

Assuming that an elite's radical credentials will affect the incidence of expropriation and the magnitude of compensation, are the sums involved sufficient to impact significantly on the overall U.S. national interest? The 1974 income earned by our Third World investments was less than $3 billion, roughly one-quarter of 1 percent of one year's national income. To put the matter still further into perspective, our investments are concentrated in relatively few developing countries. The issue, after all, is not whether the United States should be indifferent to the fate of all repressive conservative regimes, but whether we should exercise a powerful presumption on their behalf.

Furthermore, the putative threat to U.S. exports seems still less consequential. The greater part of our exports go to other developed states. The bulk of the remainder consists largely of agricultural products, arms, capital goods, and associated know-how and is, moreover, concentrated in a very few trading partners. So we find here little basis for objecting to a very much more selective approach to defining the enemy.

The size of Third World debt owed by certain right-wing governments to private financial institutions in the United States also may influence the prevailing view of radical movements. In this case too, however, the concentration of U.S. interests should, among other factors, induce a more relaxed and discriminating response. Today a mere six countries account for two-thirds of all the non-oil-exporting developing countries' obligations to banks. There is, moreover, serious doubt about the net advantage to the American economy of encouraging the export of capital at this time. Some authorities have argued that we are already experiencing a serious capital shortage.

Unbending opponents of Third World radical movements often invoke access to raw materials as one basis for their antipathy. Imports supply a significant percentage of total U.S. demand for a great variety of minerals, in part because though there may be domestic sources or substitutes, they are more expensive. One is struck, however, both by the great diversity of suppliers and the number of them that are developed states.

Unless one envisions radical revolution as a torrent restrained only by the dam of U.S. power from engulfing the entire Southern Hemisphere, this variety of sources should by itself suggest that the dimensions of the threat are rather less than we are sometimes urged to believe. Skeptics should also ask the tocsin

ringers why we should doubt that in the generality of cases, radical governments will be as anxious as conservative ones to sell their products at the best
available price. Ideology continually founders on the rock of national interest.

Moral Security

While exaggerating the threat to our national interests from a proliferation of
Marxist regimes, we have conversely failed to appreciate the full costs and risks
of intimate indiscriminate association with the Right. The cost most generally
recognized is that incurred from the impulse to bail out ideologically impecca-
ble losers. Losers are those who, as a consequence of incompetence and/or
social forces beyond their control, cannot make it on their own.

Our past efforts to rectify the natural balance of forces have incurred vast
diplomatic, financial, moral, and human loss. The easy answer to this concern,
that nothing in our generalized embrace of the Right and hostility to the Left
prevents us from cutting our losses, ignores the domestic politics of foreign
policy. Without the compelling force of a Manichaean view of international
relations, the American electorate probably will not bear the costs of a global
commitment to establish and sustain anti-Marxist governments.

In order to nourish that view of the world, the national security bureaucracy
and its political principals, buttressed by a complaisant mass media, have until
very recently winked at the abuse of human rights in conservative states while
trumpeting news of comparable delinquencies committed by Marxist regimes.
Once having stirred up an electorate always seething with evangelical emotions, elite attempts at the prudent pruning of losers encounter formidable
political obstacles.

Given the electorate's current agnosticism, my concern may seem obsolete.
But that conclusion fails to take into account the residual strength of a visceral
anticommunism which, after all, has for three decades serviced a luxurious
variety of material, social, and psychic needs.

Threat to Freedom

There arises from our insufficiently discriminating embrace of the Right a far
more serious, yet hardly noticed, peril. It is a threat not to the United States as a
participant in the game of nations, but rather to the relatively free and humane
character of its society.

Ideas are contagious. Most societies—whether of the First, Second, or Third
World—face comparable problems of alienation, class conflict, crime, ethnic
tension, inflation, and unemployment. The temptation to resolve contradictions
by suppressing them, to eliminate social tensions by annihilating one side of the
dialogue, lurks in every nation.

Any nation's commitment to an open political process rooted in the egalitarian distribution of fundamental political and civil rights needs constant reaf-
firmation. The nation's commitment weakens if its government celebrates

human rights at home while plainly assisting those who assault them abroad, even hailing the delinquents' achievement of domestic "order" and economic progress.

The potentially erosive influence on our own democratic process comes primarily from the rightist authoritarians who solicit our support and collaboration, rather than from their left-wing enemies. The latter offer solutions to the problems of modern society which rub against the grain of our national ethos and challenge an overwhelming phalanx of vested interests. The former, on the other hand, being zealously committed to traditional capitalist institutions and economic formulas, offer solutions to contemporary societal ills which promise to reenforce existing hierarchies in the name of private enterprise and individual initiative.

Thus they appeal to the self-interest of the upper and even arguably the middle classes and to the belief structure of the overwhelming majority of Americans. Moreover, having themselves chosen avenues of development which require a warm and intimate relationship with American investors and a continual flow-through of American managerial and technical personnel, they have channels for the projection of influence unavailable to regimes of the Left which are, at least, more circumspect in their dealings with American capital and more autarkic in their approach to development.

The problem is not simply one of a contagion of ideas among elites. Just as the defenders of freedom feel threatened by powerful foreign enemies of the open society, so the authoritarians who rely on our goodwill are threatened by the existence of a liberal and democratic America which will shelter their enemies, condemn their barbarities, and—by its very existence—challenge their view that capitalism requires the suspension of freedom. Hence they are bound to support forces and trends in our own society infirmly committed to democratic institutions.

Ideology and Human Rights

Does the putative distinction between Right and Left enjoy much intellectual merit? To begin with, one may reasonably doubt that the generality of right-wing autocrats has an inclination to restore freedom as, we are often told, "the regime gains more confidence in itself." "Confidence about what?" one may ask. Presumably about its success in so mutilating and intimidating the human beings and institutions of the Left—as well as those liberals and moderate conservatives who will defend human rights and unexpurgated democracy—that the desired repressive social order can be maintained with reduced public order expenditures and less offense to humanitarian constituencies in the Western democracies.

Even if such regimes could acquire the necessary confidence, despite their pursuit of harshly inegalitarian ends which tend today to generate opposition, the result would hardly be anything we might call freedom. Anyone who bothers to listen to what Chile's President Pinochet and comparable figures say and write cannot avoid discovering a contempt for democracy indistinguishable from the views of the most hardened Stalinist.

There is simply no persuasive historical basis for the conclusion that right-wing autocracies are less tenacious, more subject to erosion by the yearning for freedom, than those of the Left. Nor is there a persuasive theoretical case. A private sector within the economy does not necessarily represent a center of power and influence and independent opinion outside the reach of the government's arm. In fact, the government may be little more than the militarized arm of the private sector, or the two may be so intensely intertwined by mutual interest that no important differences of opinion can emerge. Or businessmen may exist purely at the sufferance of a military caste. Nor is it inevitable that cultural associations serve as independent centers of power, for they too can be participants in the regime or its docile servants.

Neither in precedent, such as it is, nor in theory do I find a basis for the presumptive attribution of superior moral features to regimes of the Right. What makes some regimes more tenacious and vicious than others is a function of national history, the domestic environment, the international context and, perhaps, the personality of leading figures. Ideology can make a regime more brutal where its application is peculiarly inappropriate to the particular society.

Removing Constraints

Thus ideology needs to be taken into account as one of several factors which help us to anticipate the humanitarian dimensions of a particular movement's political triumph. But like the other factors, it does not in the abstract justify a powerful presumption in favor of fascists, caudillos, and other assorted horsemen of the Right.

In the moral realm, as in the practical, there is no satisfactory alternative to considering each case on its complicated and often precarious merits. Until this modest proposition is generally accepted by Congress and the national security bureaucracy, the antiradical bias will continue to constrain American efforts to defend and promote human rights. □

READINGS SUGGESTED BY THE AUTHOR:

Clare, Michael T. *War without End*. New York: Random House, Vintage Books, 1972.

Gregg, Robert W., and Kegley, George W., Jr., eds. *After Vietnam: The Future of American Foreign Policy*. Garden City, N.Y.: Doubleday, Anchor Books, 1971.

Hoffman, Stanley. *Gulliver's Troubles or The Setting of American Foreign Policy*. New York: McGraw-Hill, 1968.

Steel, Ronald. *Pax Americana*. New York: Viking Press, 1967.

Wolfe, Charles, Jr. *United States Policy and the Third World*. Boston: Little, Brown, 1967.

UNDERSTATING THE COMMUNIST THREAT

ADDA B. BOZEMAN
Sarah Lawrence College

No analysis of the Nixon, Ford, and Carter policies on human rights and national security is possible without remembering that this country's self-view and its approaches to world affairs have long borne the imprint of two sets of ideas for which logic does not allow an easy linkage. One derives from the European heritage of constitutionalism and international law in terms of which individual civil rights are enforceable within—but not beyond—the reaches of the state's legal jurisdiction. The other model, by contrast, which was borrowed from eighteenth century philosophies of the law of nature and incorporated into the Declaration of Independence, stands for the proposition that all men everywhere are entitled to life, liberty and the pursuit of happiness and may therefore claim independence and statehood as functions of their innate right to self-determination.

Cultural Context

Questions whether a given human grouping has a demonstrable will and capacity to approximate the model of the democratic nation-state, whether its traditional life-style favors the principle of individuation, or whether its customary norms of law and administration allow for the liberty of speech or religion, have usually not been raised by policymakers. In fact, this nation's approach to international relations as well as to government is distinctly ahistorical and futuristic. Since it had staked its own destiny on the need to overcome the burden of the European past, it expected others to aspire to a similar liberation from the shackles of time.

A further closely related directive for politically relevant thought and action is the commitment, explicitly enjoined by our founding document, not to recognize culture as a determinant of man's place in society. The fact that art styles, religions, philosophies, manners, and social systems differ today as they did in the past continues to be registered and appreciated by the most casual American observer; yet this realization has not been allowed to contaminate the pseudo-religious conviction that human values and preferences are the same when it comes to politics, morality, and law. In sum, differences between civilizations are rarely being alluded to in official commentaries on civil liberties and human rights. The heritage of the common law is thus not necessarily appreciated as unique to our particular civilization.

Soviet Doctrine

These differences are clear in the case of the Soviet Union, where the determined installation of Marxist-Leninist categories of thought about law and the administration of human beings has driven underground the traditional legal values. The new doctrine, steadfastly maintained by Soviet authorities throughout the last half century, insists that human destiny is the exclusive function of material circumstances, more particularly of the continuous struggle between economic classes representing two contending methods of production. The liberal Western proposition that an individual is capable of developing ideas, values, and aspirations also outside this materially determined context is categorically denied. Indeed, individualism with its corollary of individuated rights has been regarded from Marx onward as a bourgeois illusion. Humanity, by contrast, is a legitimate concept in this vocabulary. However, it would come into its own only, Marx warned, when men ceased to think and feel as individuals with separate inalienable rights.

Marxism-Leninism does not recognize "natural law"; it rejects the contractual theory of the state. In official theory all law is but the will of the dominant class which holds power in the state in a particular historical epoch of the development of the forces of production—a definition that explains why "constitutionalism" is understood in this world as the dictatorship of the capitalist class. These negative understandings of what the West accepts as major positive norms and values condition all intellectually crucial human dispositions and thought processes in the Soviet Union. However, the negatives are viewed as positives by the Communist tacticians of strife when the local situation invites a psychological or political takeover; for in such an eventuality a democracy provides the ideal tools for acquiring power by allowing freedom of speech and assembly.

All communications with the Soviet Union, including the discernment of communist realities in the area of law, rights, and constitutionalism, are further impeded by the spurious, largely uncontested utilization of Western vocabularies for the conveyance of Marxist-Leninist propositions that are antithetical to the original meanings carried by the words. Notwithstanding all official strictures against the state, law, and democracy as bourgeois entrapments, the Soviet Union is yet supplied with a constitution and with law codes, all formulated on Western models. These enumerate the classical freedoms of speech, religion, assembly, and the right to demonstrate, but they also stipulate that these political rights may be exercised by citizens only in order to strengthen the established order. They may under no circumstances be advanced against the state, for the ruling assumption is that rights are granted by the state. And since this state is also authoritatively defined by its spokesmen as a dictatorship of the proletariat functioning under the leadership of the Communist party, it is an illusion to believe that civil or political rights are recognized by the Soviet Union.

The situation is somewhat different when it comes to so-called social, economic, and cultural rights, if only because the Soviet Union is ideologically committed to provide its peoples with social security, public health services, education, and work. Impressive achievements have been registered under these headings, albeit at a cost that nontotalitarian societies would not be willing to pay.

Ideology and Conflict

The steady expansion and consolidation of the Marxist-Leninist ideology in all parts of the world, and the Soviet Union's establishment of firm political and military controls over the territories of once independent states in Eastern and central Europe, present analysts of the human factor in Soviet-American relations with another set of questions that require at least cursory attention before one can decide first, whether there is a category of universally accepted human rights in terms of which Soviet dispositions to rights can be faulted on legal or moral grounds, and second, what policy options are open to the United States when a situation calls for "interference" or "expressions of concern."

The original legal recognition of individual rights as well as group rights occurred everywhere within the contours of the state. However, in Marxist-Leninist doctrine and hence also in the practice of modern Communist states, the state as norm is devoid of jural or any other definitive significance. Accepted as a temporary tactical convenience in the evolution toward a world communist society to be organized along wholly different lines, it is as much subject to arbitrary interventions on the part of humanity's Communist guardians as is the individual.

All state-centered political designs are thus fraught by ambiguities today, and the same is true of such relatively new syndromes of allegedly universally valid norms as a people's right to self-determination. This was as important to Woodrow Wilson as it was to Lenin. But whereas such a potential defiance of the established political order was viewed by Wilson as the necessary prelude to the achievement of national freedom and sovereignty by minority peoples in Eastern Europe and the Near East, it was envisioned by Lenin as a device to pry all dissatisfied or freedom-seeking groups—among them in particular minorities and colonial peoples—loose from the jurisdiction of the bourgeois order of things so as to ready them through agitation, propaganda, and manipulation for their historic roles as fighters for the camp of socialism and against the camp of capitalism.

This fight has ever since been conducted by the Soviet Union and its surrogate or allied forces with admirable steadfastness of purpose and in strict accordance with the programs and rules of the Communist party's operational code—each and all well known by the Soviet Union's friends and enemies. American policies, by contrast, have lacked long-range perspectives and were no match for the Communist design. The influence and power of the United States were thus progressively eroded, and in some cases eliminated outright, by the skillful blend of diplomacy and warfare which its Communist rival invested year in, year out, in such strategically vital areas as east central Europe and Southeast Asia. National noncommunist governments in these lands could thus be replaced by communist regimes; indigeneous populations were pronounced liberated, and the case for self-determination was considered closed.

The last massive transformation of this kind has been administered by Soviet supported forces in Vietnam, Laos, and Cambodia after the Communist takeover in 1975. It has been, and continues to be, conducted without regard for the rights of man, individuated or collective, and at a staggering cost of human life. This entire complex of unredeemed human suffering—which is covered by the term "the human factor"—is today totally removed from American policy considerations. It evidently does not call for "interference," and it even seems to have ceased being a matter of "legitimate international concern." The only "human" factor that interests the defeated United States as it readies itself for the opening of friendly relations with its victors are the whereabouts of the human remains of Americans still considered missing in action.

Relations with Eastern Europe

Our present reaction to violations of human rights in the Communist states of Eastern and central Europe is different for a variety of reasons, chief among them the following. This area, being territorially contiguous to the Russian landmass, is militarily, politically, and economically so tightly controlled by the Soviet Union that it may legitimately be viewed as part of the new Russian imperium. Our relations with the nominally independent sovereign states in the Soviet bloc are therefore in most important respects also aspects of our relations with the Soviet Union.

Second, the North-South galaxy of Eastern European states—from which Estonia, Latvia, and Lithuania are excluded after their incorporation into the

Soviet federation of republics—is also territorially contiguous to what now stands as Western Europe, the region west of the line dividing Germany, historically the heartland of the continent. American security interests are thus centered in this rump of a critically divided Europe. Today this nation is absolutely dependent on its cultural motherland, the one that had originated the concepts of civil liberties and the rights of man.

However, the proposition that political security and consciousness of culture are closely linked, and that American security interests are therefore well served if a foreign nation's civilization is thoroughly understood, is not congenial to official American opinion. The neglect of this particular dimension of "the human factor" is well illustrated by the circumstances during and after World War II in which the failure of American planning, and our unfamiliarity with the Soviet ideological and philosophical orientation, allowed the Baltic states, Poland, parts of Germany, Czechoslavakia, Hungary, and Yugoslavia to pass behind the Iron Curtain. This failure in planning and foresight, which is the ultimate cause of our continuing security crisis and the raison d'être, therefore, of the conferences in Helsinki in 1975 and Belgrade in 1977, has very much to do with our disregard of the cultural and historical component in the configuration of modern states.

What we choose to forget is that generations of peoples in that broad north-south belt stretching from Finland to the Adriatic Sea have lived west of a most important line separating communities Christianized by Rome from those Christianized by Constantinople. Prominent among the latter are the Russians who succeeded to the imperial Byzantine tradition before experiencing that of their Mongolian conquerors, and who were left untouched by the great movement of the Renaissance. Prominent among the former are Baltic groups, Poles, Germans, Bohemians, Hungarians, Croats, and others who participated for centuries in the political, moral, and legal system which constitutes Western Europe's civilization, and who know therefore what individual civil liberties are. It is here, then, that revolts have been occurring continuously since 1948.

These reflections permit the following conclusions on the contentious subject of political liberties in American-Soviet relations. (1) Civil rights were not internationally enforceable norms in the classical international law that regulated relations between the sovereign nation-states of the morally and legally unified West. (2) These rights do not constitute the shared understandings of the role of the individual in society in today's multicultural, ideologically disunited world. (3) Desuetude is the lot today of most core norms identified with international law, notably those recited most frequently in charters and treaties. Quite in counterpoint to all the unifying structures built of words, we must thus count today with the existence of divergent—in most respects legally and morally incompatible—systems of thought and organization.

In this situation it cannot be maintained that the absence or violation of individuated political rights in the Soviet Union constitutes a legal cause for intervention by the United States. However, it is most certainly a matter of legitimate concern, both morally and politically, nowhere more so than in Eastern Europe. Intervention on this ground, which implies considerations of our own national interests, is entirely fathomable; but it would have to be predicated on the admission that the paper order of the international system, being now devoid of meaning, is no longer binding on the West.

International Environment

American concerns with the human factor in foreign relations are being conveyed today by references to "human rights" rather than to civil or political rights. However, the essence of the latter has to be borne in mind if the former are to be understood. Contrary to the rights stipulated, for example, in the American Bill of Rights, human rights are, by definition, universal. It is therefore no coincidence that their elaboration is closely related to the establishment and evolution of the United Nations. A reading of the relevant charter provisions, declarations, covenants, and committee and council resolutions shows furthermore that attention centers on collective or group rather than individual rights, and that the stress is on economic, social, and cultural rights.

This shift away from individuated rights and the consequent formulation of group rights is properly viewed as a diplomatic victory for the Soviet Union, but it also mirrors certain diplomatic realities. Too many group rights are incompatible with respect for individuated political rights, if only because they represent the policy objectives of the state. Furthermore, the so-called "programme rights" of the Covenant on Economic, Social, and Cultural Rights are subject to discretionary governmental implementation. Governments ratifying the covenant are merely asked to report what they have done or what they intend to achieve, and since most of today's governments are authoritarian, it is not difficult to agree with John P. Humphrey's conclusion that "more and more the individual stands alone in the face of an all-pervading State." Furthermore, and contrary to an earlier international consensus, concern for the rights of minorities has been steadily decreasing in the United Nations.

In short, the human rights vocabulary is marked by ambiguity and imprecision. It invites political, not legal, discourse and sanctions capricious conduct on the part of local and international authorities because it does not provide objective jural standards for the definition of rights and their violations. Reliable procedures for the handling of human rights complaints—and these come yearly from thousands of individuals—cannot even be expected in the heavily politicized circumstances that are being condoned in the human rights commissions of the United Nations and the various non-European regions.

The phrase "human rights" does not refer to legal propositions or to realities as these are perceivable today. In its most positive meaning it constitutes a list of desires, political goals, or ideological commitments. Read negatively, but equally justifiably, it may be likened to a paper blanket covering up the absence of real and enforceable rights of the kind customary under Western constitutionalism.

Ford, Carter, and Helsinki

Security interests in our relationship with the Soviet bloc should not be carried out by confidence in human rights provisions written under the auspices of the United Nations. The opposite is suggested by the record of foreign policy pronouncements in the Ford and Carter administrations. These are heavy with references to international law, legal commitments, and the compelling demands of a universally valid code of morality; they are light in explanations as to just how this particular type of concern with human rights is linked to the security interests of the nation.

The Helsinki Agreement among the United States, the Soviet Union, thirty-two European states, and Turkey issued from the Helsinki Conference on Security and Cooperation in Europe in 1975. The texts of speeches by former President Ford concerning the agreement are replete with ambiguities. For example, after referring to the signatories' "diverse cultures," Ford yet reminded the peoples of the East "that the principles on which the Conference had agreed are part of the great heritage of European civilization which we all hold in trust for all mankind." Just how are we to understand the reasoning that underlies this conviction? Does our government really assume that all mankind is morally unified around principles *also* found in European civilization, or does it believe that the representatives of Europe's civilization are the trustees of this particular heritage, charged with educating the rest of mankind?

In aligning itself firmly with these positions on human rights—illogical as they may seem to be—and in expanding the radius of their relevance to the world-at-large, the Carter administration has so far compounded existing confusions. These aspects of the human rights policy as pursued by the Ford and Carter administrations must be viewed, regrettably, as symptoms of a serious crisis in our capacity to conceptualize the problems of human existence with which our foreign policy is challenged to deal. This crisis, the most serious faced by the nation today, will not be solved by rushing into evangelistic prose and building paper façades of solemn covenants and pledges for what Ivor Richards has termed "camouflaging realities."

The security problems implicit in our relationship with the Soviet Union have been greatly aggravated by the present self-induced crisis in thought and language use. The Helsinki Agreement thus sanctions the coexistence of two mutually exclusive conceptions of the European order and the world society. On the one hand, it assumes the existence of an international community of individuals, with each and all entitled to the enjoyment of the same human rights. On the other hand, the Final Act confirms the continued validity of ths classical vocabulary of international law and the states system, in the context of which each state is fully sovereign within its domestic jurisdiction. This paradox is confounded by the fact that the two major signatories of the Helsinki document differ in their interpretation of its meaning and purport.

Détente

But the major premise for the American participation in the Helsinki conference and for the ratification—however tacit—of Europe's existing boundaries was the national commitment to détente in relations with the Soviet Union. In the language of the American administrations, and therefore also in the nation's interpretation of all official references to détente, the word is practically synonymous with peace; and peace, again, is generally understood as the opposite of war as well as conflict. In Communist usage, by contrast, détente means something entirely different. In the present historical era détente has been authoritatively defined by Brezhnev:

> Détente does not in the slightest abolish, and cannot abolish or alter, the laws of the class struggle. No one should expect that, because of détente, Communists will reconcile themselves to capitalist exploitation.

Détente, then, is not a synonym for "peaceful coexistence," and "peaceful coexistence" is not a dimension of peace as generally understood in the West.

Why was the American public made to believe that peace and détente—the two major references in the Helsinki Agreement—are international givens, in no need of explanation? Should the signatories of the Final Act not have registered their full awareness of the fact that these two words have totally different connotations in the East and the West? The leaders of the West, perhaps notably of the United States, have much to learn in this respect from the spokesmen for the Soviet Union who have been consistently clear, from the days of Lenin onward, in their instructions to friends and adversaries alike, just how détente relates to peace, and in which ways both serve Soviet conceptions of tactics, strategy, and security.

A definitive assessment of Helsinki and subsequent developments in our foreign policies may be premature, but it is difficult to agree with Ford's rationalization of the Helsinki arrangements: that "if it all fails, Europe will be no worse off than it is now." Washington may have thought of Helsinki as "a modest undertaking," but its implications for Warsaw, Prague, or East Berlin are surely more serious than that, and the same holds for the governments and peoples of Western Europe.

The difference here may well be a function of different orientations toward time, specifically perhaps to experiences recorded in the past. No one in Europe will forget either the uprisings and protests against Communist totalitarianism in Poland, East Germany, Hungary, or Czechoslovakia, or the skillful integration of ideology, military force, and semantic prowess that marked the crushing of these national and individual activities in furtherance of "the dignity of man." Nor has the fact been consigned to oblivion that the United States was

politically and militarily passive in the decades that climaxed in the years 1968
and 1970, even though it had morally and verbally encouraged this stubborn
Eastern European resistance. Is our latest or our "new" initiative in behalf of
human rights in this tortured European world designed to be more credible?

The American ratification of détente at Helsinki has provided the Soviet
Union with many opportunities for furthering its objectives in economic development, political consolidation, and diplomacy; it has not been instrumental in
promoting the cause of primary human rights. Certain technical provisions,
calling—among other measures—for harmonizing statistical standards, arrang-
ing uniform hotel classifications, and promoting medical cooperation between
the signatory states, may have been implemented. But it would surely be
extravagant to regard these arrangements of Basket III as "rights," or as
stepping-stones toward the gradual evolution of legal norms protective of
human dignity or conducive to "the spiritual enrichment of the personality."

However, in encouraging protests and inducing a certain edginess on the part
of the ruling agencies, our Helsinki policy has been effective in baring the
vulnerability of the Soviet Union on several counts: it has revealed the lack of
progress in intellectual life and culture, and, above all, it has removed whatever
cover-ups remained from the realities of deep human disaffection with the
Soviet order. Yet these effects of Helsinki and its aftermath have not, and
probably will not, be translated into advantages for our side because we lack the
necessary policy design. There is thus no counterforce to stem the measures of
repression against dissidence which have become intensified in the last few
years.

The present human rights situation in the signatory states of Eastern Europe is
infinitely more complex than that in the predominantly Russian realm. The
main reasons for this difference must be sought in the realm's culture and
history on one hand, and in the satellite status of the nations on the other.
Helsinki has sparked protest after protest here, nowhere more so than in the
region's northern triangle of East Germany, Poland, and Czechoslovakia,
which constitute the foremost advance bastion of the Russian empire and are
securely held by hundreds of thousands of Soviet troops. Despite forbidding
odds, people here have not ceased being rebellious. It would be unreasonable,
however, to overestimate Eastern Europe's capacity to withstand Russian
pressures.

Helsinki Fallout

Evaluating the effect of the American Helsinki initiative upon the nation's
own processes of foreign policy making can only be tentative, but reasons exist
to make one skeptical of President Carter's decision to make the Helsinki
guidelines applicable to all nations everywhere, irrespective of whether our
security concerns are served or damaged by such a move. The Ford administration, being ideologically less doctrinaire than its successor, was more cautious

and reflective in this regard. However, spokesmen for the present administration, including President Carter, have since modified the message and the tone so that it is difficult today to know in just which ways our policy toward the Soviet Union diverges from our policies toward other nations, friendly or unfriendly. This means that the security issue is being made to fade from public consciousness. It also means that we cannot focus clearly on the preestablished either-or of "interference" or "legitimate international concern."

Last year, when I had my first chance to think seriously about Helsinki, I was more optimistic, even though I had to register several reservations. Some of the conclusions which I reached then I still hold to today:

- Human rights are not legally firm propositions, either in domestic or international law.
- Human rights are not morally shared values or norms throughout the world.
- Human rights are legitimate concerns, not internationally or transnationally but nationally and culturally in the context of Western civilization.
- Human rights are legitimate policy propositions, and as such require profound study before they are entrusted to diplomacy.

Has the West, under the leadership of the United States, at long last found a way of countering Communist ideological offensives by developing its own ideological initiatives, and if this should be so, is it likely that this new human rights diplomacy will succeed?

Assessing our human rights policy two years after Helsinki does not allow for the conclusion that we have formulated a coherent strategic design, or that we have an equivalent for the Soviet doctrine of "the corelation of forces"—a term which includes the aggregate of psychological, intellectual, military, political, and economic forces bearing on a given situation. Hopes to substantiate such a design in Soviet-American relations will therefore have to be deferred until we come to realize that security in the moral, political, and military sense is, in the final analysis, a function of an enduring national will.☐

READINGS SUGGESTED BY THE AUTHOR:

Bozeman, Adda B. *The Future of Law in a Multicultural World*. Princeton, N.J.: Princeton University Press, 1971.

Cranston, Maurice. *What Are Human Rights?* New York: Basic Books, 1962.

Humphrey, John P. "The World Revolution and Human Rights." In *Human Rights, Federalism, and Minorities*, edited by Allan E. Gotlieb. Contemporary Affairs Series No. 43. Toronto: Canadian Institute of International Affairs, 1970.

Marshall, Charles Burton. *American Foreign Policy as a Dimension of the American Revolution*. Washington, D.C.: American Enterprise Institute for Public Policy Research, 1974.

CONTINUITY AND CHANGE IN AMERICAN FOREIGN POLICY

HENRY A. KISSINGER
Former Secretary of State

Delivering a "major appraisal" of current American foreign policy presents
me with a dilemma—a difficult choice between public interest in the
subject on the one hand and the imperatives of responsibility on the other.
Despite my notorious humility, it would be tempting for me to speculate about
how I might have dealt with this or that tactical situation if I had been in office
these past ten months. But those who have borne the responsibility of high
office know too well the complexities, ambiguities, and anguish of charting our
nation's course in a turbulent period. The new administration deserves the
opportunity to develop its policies without harassment or second-guessing. Ten
months is, after all, but an instant in the life of nations.

President Carter and Secretary of State Vance are on the verge of delicate and
important negotiations—with the Soviet Union on strategic arms limitation,
with the Middle East foreign ministers on peace in that crucial area, and with
other leaders attending the United Nations General Assembly on a variety of
complex issues. The hopes of *all* Americans go with them. The success of the
administration in promoting peace and progress will be a success for the nation.
Any setbacks of the administration would affect the lives and prosperity of all
Americans. When a performer is taking careful and complicated steps on a high
wire, it is profoundly inappropriate, not to say dangerous, for a spectator in a
seat far below to shout at him that he is putting his toe in the wrong place.

So I would like to discuss some of the philosophical underpinnings from which tactical decisions derive: the nature and purpose of bipartisanship in our democracy; the challenge of pursuing our moral values, especially human rights, in a complex world; and the relationship of issues such as human rights to others, the so-called problem of linkage.

Nature of Bipartisanship

The world marvels at the United States's extraordinary rebound from the agony of Vietnam and the constitutional crisis of Watergate. We have emerged from these traumas with our democratic institutions flourishing, our public debates vigorous, our economy expanding, our pride in our country intact. Our friends around the world were heartened by this, for they know better perhaps even than we do how vital a stake they have in the United States's confident leadership.

That leadership is not—nor should it be—the esoteric concern of specialists; it is the means by which the nation serves its interests and pursues its highest goals, and it affects all other nations. For thirty years the world balance of power, the cohesion of the democracies, the health of the world economy, the prospects for growth in Africa, Asia, and Latin America, and the hopes for freedom everywhere have been sustained by the United States.

We have learned through many crises that upheavals thousands of miles away can threaten American lives or jeopardize American prosperity. The 1973 Middle East war ultimately forced us into a military alert. The oil embargo, lasting six months, cost half a million jobs and $10 billion in national output; it set the stage for a serious recession, in this country and worldwide. And the abrupt quadrupling of oil prices which followed added at least five percentage points to the price index, contributing to our worst inflation since World War II. We have not yet returned to the high growth rate and relatively low inflation which we enjoyed before 1973.

Now that the bitter passions of the foreign policy debate of the last ten years are hopefully behind us, it is time for thoughtful deliberation on what are, or should be, our basic premises about the world in which we find ourselves today. Our foreign policy difficulties are often described as the legacy of Vietnam. But the Vietnam ordeal was not a cause but a symptom. The late 1960s, coinciding with Vietnam, marked the end of the period when the United States was overwhelmingly more powerful than any other nation, when we could assault problems alone and entirely with our own resources, when American initiatives were accepted without serious debate, when we could believe that our own domestic experiences, like the New Deal, were the automatic blueprint for economic development and political progress abroad. It marked above all the end of the era when we could imagine that any problem could be resolved once and for all and that solutions once achieved would permit us to end our international exertions.

Vietnam was a catharsis. It taught us that our power—while great—is finite, that our influence—though crucial—can be effective only if we understand our priorities and the world in which we live. For a century and a half geography and resources combined to give us the luxury of waiting until threats became almost overwhelming before we committed ourselves. We always had the opportunity to compensate for our tardy involvement by the massive deployment of physical power. We could largely leave to others the burden of the day-to-day decisions that over time spelled war or peace, security or fear, for the global system and even for ourselves. We were spared the continuing agony of inescapable decisions that other nations always faced to assure their survival and their values. More than any other nation in history, we could avoid the dilemma of reconciling the ideal with the practical, of accommodating to limited means and contingent ends.

The post-World War II era was a remarkably creative period of American foreign policy. But our initiatives were explicitly justified as temporary measures to restore an underlying equilibrium. The Marshall Plan, our alliance commitments overseas, our international economic programs, were all conceived as dealing with temporary emergencies which once overcome would excuse us from permanent direct involvement abroad.

The world of today is not the world of a generation ago. Geography no longer assures security. The American nuclear monopoly has given way to nuclear balance and to proliferating weapons capabilities. The United States is now as vulnerable as any other nation; indeed, nuclear weapons confront all peoples everywhere with a threat to their survival unknown to any previous generation.

The world economy has become interdependent; our prosperity is to some extent hostage to the decisions on raw materials, prices, and investment in distant countries whose purposes are not necessarily compatible with ours. And the structure of relations between nations has fundamentally altered. In 1945 fifty-one nations joined to create the United Nations; today it comprises nearly 150 nations—many ideologically hostile. Just as two world wars shattered the Europe-oriented order of the last two centuries, so the postwar system of Cold War bipolarity has come apart—and a new pattern of world order must be shaped to take its place.

An increasing responsibility has fallen upon the United States. Without our commitment to international security, there can be no stable peace; without our constructive participation in the world economy, there can be no hope for economic progress; without our dedication to human liberty, the prospect of freedom in the world is dim indeed. For the first time in American history we can neither dominate the world nor escape from it. Henceforth this country will be engaged in world affairs by reality and not by choice. The United States must now learn to conduct foreign policy as other nations have had to conduct it—with patience, subtlety, imagination, and perseverance.

The most fundamental challenge is thus not to our physical resources but to our constancy of purpose and our philosophical perception. Precisely because we can no longer wait for dangers to become overwhelming, they will appear ambiguous when they are still manageable. The case for ratifying the Panama Canal treaties, for example, is not an immediate present danger in Panama but the need to forestall a united front of *all* the countries of Latin America against what they consider an American attempt to maintain inequity by force. The issue in Angola two years ago was not a direct threat to our security, but the long-term danger of allowing Soviet surrogate forces to intervene globally to tip the scales in local conflicts. The argument for a forthcoming American attitude in the North-South dialogue is not to yield to the admittedly limited strength of the less developed nations, but to prevent the polarization of the world into a small minority of the rich isolated in an ocean of poverty and resentment.

It is a paradox of the contemporary world that if we wait until these dangers become realities we will lose the chance to do anything about them. At the moment when we still have great scope for creativity, the facts are likely to be unclear or ambiguous. When we know all the facts, it is often too late to act. This is the dilemma of statesmanship of a country that is irrevocably engaged in world affairs—and particularly of one that seeks to lead.

The United States, therefore, can no longer afford the luxury of oscillating as it once did between brooding isolation and crusading intervention. Our biggest foreign policy challenge is to shape a concept of our international role that the American people will support over the long term; we must avoid dramatic swings between exuberance and abdication. Our responsibility is unending; our accomplishments are likely to be ever tenuous. We must change our approach to international affairs from the episodic to the permanent, from the belief in final answers to the realization that each "solution" is only an admission ticket to a new set of problems.

In such an environment the conduct of foreign policy requires a fine balance between continuity and change. This is not easy for our democracy. Our two-party system, our constitutionally mandated balancing and separation of powers, our open political process, create temptations for the simplified answer, the nostalgic withdrawal, or the moralistic sense of superiority.

Yet this free and open political process is also our greatest source of strength. The alternation of parties in office by free elections guarantees constant renewal, the infusion of fresh ideas and new blood into our national life. It presents a striking contrast with the gerontocracies that run the Communist world. These systems have no lawful regular process for replacing leaders; it is no coincidence that the stagnation of their aging leadership goes hand-in-hand with plodding bureaucracy and intellectual sterility, punctuated by periodic crises over succession.

The problem which our society faces is on the whole a far happier one. Insuring continuity amidst the constant process of renewal turns bipartisanship from a slogan into an imperative. To be sure, all administrations sooner or later appeal to the spirit of bipartisanship. This is partly because they come to share much the same perception of the nation's permanent interests as their predecessors, and partly because bipartisanship can be a useful shield against excessive criticism. There is a natural tendency for the party in power to consider *any* criticism as excessive. I know these tendencies from experience, having indulged them myself. But the fact that there are also tactical benefits to the appeal to bipartisanship does not change the reality that to the world at large we are one nation which can have only one government.

And we are not just *any* nation. Our country cannot uproot its whole foreign policy every four or eight years—or imply that it is doing so—or else the United States will itself become a major factor of instability in the world. We must understand that foreign leaders who design their programs around our policies are staking their domestic positions on our constancy. Radical shifts in our course inevitably affect the stability of especially friendly governments. If these changes are seen to occur largely for domestic effect, if our elections come to determine as well the stability of foreign governments, no nation that has a choice will readily cooperate with us.

Of course a foreign policy that stresses continuity above all else would be stultifying and would in time be overwhelmed by events. A new administration is obviously not elected to carry out all the policies of its predecessor. But change in our policy should be seen as reflecting new circumstances and not change for its own sake. By the same token, critics have an obligation to see to it that our foreign policy debates reflect disagreements on major substance, not a quest for partisan advantage or tactical second-guessing.

If our foreign policy is well conceived, it must reflect fundamental national purposes and not personal idiosyncrasy. Neither the administration nor the opposition should nurture differences to score debating points. Both have an obligation to make clear that our foreign policy is a shared national enterprise. I might add parenthetically that bipartisanship would come easier if each new administration resisted the quadrennial temptation of implying that conceptual insight, creativity, and moral awareness begin anew every four years on January 20. Nor should history be rewritten in ways more suitable to faculty debates than to serious national dialogue.

The administration, when it pursues the national interest, is entitled to the full measure of support from all who cherish the future of the country. For its challenges are great. The new administration assumed responsibility when hopeful progress was being made in most areas of foreign policy—the Middle East, SALT, relations with both the industrialized and the developing world. But it faces a tremendous task in each, and in continuing to shape the new international order. We are on a journey no single administration can possibly complete, whose beginning is an understanding of reality and whose goal is a better and more peaceful life for future generations.

Morality and Pragmatism

In this spirit I would now like to turn to one of the basic challenges of foreign policy, the perennial tension between morality and pragmatism. Whenever it has been forced to wield its great power, the United States has also been driven to search its conscience. How does our foreign policy serve moral ends? How can the United States carry out its role as humane example and champion of justice in a world in which power is still often the final arbiter? How do we reconcile ends and means, principle and survival? How do we keep secure both our existence *and* our values? These have been the moral and intellectual dilemmas of the United States for two hundred years.

From the time of the Declaration of our Independence, Americans have believed that this country has a moral significance for the world. The United States was created as a conscious act by men and women dedicated to a set of political and ethical principles they held to be of universal meaning. Small wonder, then, that Santayana declared that "being an American is, of itself, almost a moral condition."

At the same time, since Tocqueville it has been observed that we are a pragmatic people, commonsensical, undogmatic, undoctrinaire—a nation with a permanent bent to the practical and an instinct for what works. We have defined our basic goals—justice, freedom, equality, and progress—in open and libertarian terms, seeking to enlarge opportunity and the human spirit rather than to coerce a uniform standard of behavior or a common code of doctrine and belief.

This duality of our nature is *not* at war with reality. For in international politics our morality and power should not be antithetical. Any serious foreign policy must begin with the need for survival. And survival has its practical, necessities. A nation does not willingly delegate control over its future. For a great power to remit its security to the mercy of others is an abdication of foreign policy. All serious foreign policy therefore begins with maintaining a balance of power—a scope for action, a capacity to affect events and conditions. Without that capacity a nation is reduced to striking empty poses.

But, equally, our nation cannot rest its policy on power alone. Our tradition and the values of our people ensure that a policy that seeks only to manipulate force would lack all conviction, consistency, and public support. This is why the United States has been most successful in our relations with the world when we combined our idealism and our pragmatism—from the days when our Founding Fathers manipulated the monarchical rivalries of Europe to secure our independence and launch the great democratic experiment to the creative American initiatives after the Second World War such as the Marshall Plan. Our modern efforts to achieve strategic arms limitation, peace in the Middle East and southern Africa, the opening to China, recasting international economic relations based on the principle of interdependence—these have also served both moral and practical ends and can be sustained only by a combination of moral conviction and practical wisdom.

Enhancing Human Rights

These considerations come to bear powerfully on the question of the relationship between human rights and foreign policy. The world needs to know what this country stands for. But we cannot rest on this; we must know how to implement our convictions and achieve an enhancement of human rights *together* with other national objectives. Neither the issue nor the concern are new:

- It was under the two previous administrations that Jewish emigration from the Soviet Union was raised from 400 a year in 1968 to 35,000 by 1973. This resulted from a deliberate policy, as a concomitant to the process of improving American-Soviet relations.
- The release of the courageous Soviet dissident Bukovsky in exchange for the Chilean Communist leader imprisoned in Chile was arranged in 1976 through American intercession. It was but one of many such acts which were not publicized in order to be able to continue to assist hardship cases.
- American diplomatic action in the same period brought about the release of hundreds of prisoners from jails all over the world.
- American foreign policy of the past decade helped enshrine basic principles of human rights in the Final Act of the Helsinki Conference on Security and Cooperation in Europe—providing the indispensable political and legal basis for pursuing the issue of human rights in East-West relations.
- We also worked to improve the efforts of the United Nations Human Rights Commission and to upgrade the Commission on Human Rights of the Organization of American States. Common human rights policies were forged with the other democracies, and steps were taken to improve the institutional response of the international system to the challenge of human rights.

The accomplishment of the new administration is not that it originated the concern with human rights, but that free of the legacy of Vietnam and Watergate it has seized the opportunity to endow the policy with a more explicit formulation. The aim of the Carter administration has been to give the American people, after the traumas of Vietnam and Watergate, a renewed sense of the basic decency of this country, so that they may continue to have the pride and self-confidence to remain actively involved in the world.

Having had to conduct American foreign policy in a period of national division and self-flagellation, I applaud and support this objective. The president has tapped a wellspring of American patriotism, idealism, unity, and commitment which are vital to our country and to the world. He has focused public concern on one of the greatest blights of our time.

The modern age has brought undreamt-of benefits to mankind—in medicine, in scientific and technological advance, and in communication. But the modern age has also spawned new tools of oppression and of civil strife. Terrorism and bitter ideological contention have weakened bonds of social cohesion; the yearning for order even at the expense of liberty has resulted all too often in the violation of fundamental standards of human decency.

The central moral problem of government has always been to strike a just and effective balance between freedom and authority. When freedom degenerates into anarchy, the human personality becomes subject to arbitrary, brutal, and capricious forces—witness aberrations of terrorism in even the most humane societies. Yet when the demand for order overrides all other considerations, man becomes a means and not an end, a tool of impersonal machinery. Human rights are the very essence of a meaningful life, and human dignity is the ultimate purpose of civil governments. Respect for the rights of man is written into the founding documents of almost every nation of the world. It has long been part of the common speech and daily lives of our citizens.

The obscene and atrocious acts systematically employed to devalue, debase, and destroy man during World War II vividly and ineradicably impressed on the world the enormity of the challenge to human rights. It was to end such abuses and to provide moral authority in international affairs that new institutions and legal standards were forged after that war—globally in the United Nations and in this hemisphere in a strengthened inter-American system.

The fact remains that continuing practices of intimidation, terror, and brutal-ity, fostered sometimes from outside national territories and sometimes from inside, mark the distance yet to be traveled before the community of nations can claim that it is truly civilized. This is why the distinguished junior senator from New York, Senator Moynihan, is surely right in stressing that human rights should be not simply a humanitarian program but a *political* component of American foreign policy.

For the difference between freedom and totalitarianism is not transient or incidental; it is a moral conflict, of fundamental historical proportions, which gives the modern age its special meaning and peril. Our defense of human rights reminds us of the fundamental reason that our competition with totalitarian systems is vital to the cause of mankind. There is no reason for us to accept the hypocritical double standard increasingly prevalent in the United Nations where petty tyrannies berate us for our alleged moral shortcomings. On this issue we are not—and have no reason to be—on the defensive. "The cause of human liberty," the poet Archibald MacLeish has written, "is now the one great revolutionary cause."

And yet, while human rights must be an essential component of our foreign policy, to pursue it effectively over the long term we must take the measure of the dangers and dilemmas along the way. First, any foreign policy must ultimately be judged by its operational results. "In foreign relations," Walter Lippmann once wrote, "as in all other relations, a policy has been formed only when commitments and power have been brought into balance."

To be sure, the advocacy of human rights has in itself a political and even strategic significance. But in the final reckoning more than advocacy will be counted. If we universalize our human rights policy, applying it indiscriminatingly and literally to all countries, we run the risk of becoming the world's policeman—an objective the American people may not support. At a minimum we will have to answer what may be the question for several friendly governments: how and to what extent we will support them if they get into difficulties by following our maxims. And we will have to indicate what sanctions we will apply to less well-disposed governments which challenge the very precepts of our policy.

If, on the other hand, we confine ourselves to proclaiming objectives that are not translated into concrete actions and specific results, we run the risk of demonstrating that we are impotent and of evoking a sense of betrayal among those our human rights policy seeks to help. Such a course could tempt unfriendly governments to crack down all the harder on their dissidents, in order to demonstrate the futility of our proclamations—this indeed has already happened to some extent in the Soviet Union.

Nor can we escape from the dilemma by asserting that there is no connection between human rights behavior and our attitude on other foreign policy problems—by "unlinking," as the technical phrase goes, human rights from other issues. For this implies that there is no cost or consequence to the violation of human rights, turning our proclamation of human rights into a liturgical theme—decoupled, unenforced, and compromised. Or else we will insist on our values only against weaker countries, in Latin America or Asia, many of which may even be conducting foreign policies supportive of our own. This would lead to the paradox that the weaker the nation and the less its importance on the international scene, the firmer and more uncompromising would be our human rights posture.

Second, precisely because human rights advocacy is a powerful political weapon, we must be careful that in its application we do not erode all moral dividing lines. We must understand the difference between governments making universal ideological claims and countries which do not observe all democratic practices—either because of domestic turmoil, foreign danger, or national traditions—but which make no claim to historical permanence or universal relevance. In the contemporary world it is the totalitarian systems which have managed the most systematic and massive repression of human rights.

In recent decades no totalitarian regime has ever evolved into a democracy. Several authoritarian regimes—such as Spain, Greece, and Portugal—have done so. We must therefore maintain the moral distinction between aggressive totalitarianism and other governments which with all their imperfections are trying to resist foreign pressures or subversion and which thereby help preserve the balance of power in behalf of all free peoples. Our human rights policy owes special consideration to the particular international and domestic setting of governments important to our security and supportive of free world security interests.

There are, of course, some transgressions of human rights which no necessity—real or imagined—can justify. But there are also realities in the threats nations face, either from terrorism at home such as in Argentina or aggression across borders such as Iran or Korea. And we must keep in mind that the alternative to some governments that resist totalitarianism with authoritarian methods may not be greater democracy and an enhancement of human rights but the advent of even more repression, more brutality, more suffering. The ultimate irony would be a posture of resignation toward totalitarian states and harassment of those who would be our friends and who have every prospect of evolving in a more humane direction.

We must take care, finally, that our affirmation of human rights is not manipulated by our political adversaries to isolate countries whose security is important for the future of freedom, even if their domestic practices fall short of our maxims. The membership of the UN Human Rights Commission, composed as it is of a number of nations with extremely dubious human rights practices, does not augur well for an objective approach to this issue in the United Nations. Cuba and other Communist governments, as well as the more repressive regimes of the less developed world, have no moral standing to bring other nations to international account. We should not hesitate to say so.

Third, there is the ominous prospect that the issue of human rights if not handled with great wisdom could unleash new forces of American isolationism. This could defeat the administration's goal of using it to mobilize support for continued American involvement in world affairs. That the human rights issue could develop a life of its own, regardless of the administration's prudent sense of its aims and limits, is already evident from some developments in Congress.

A distorted or misunderstood human rights policy can become the basis and justification of a modern isolationism. What appeals to many as a useful impetus to resistance to the Communist challenge can be used by others to erase all the distinctions between totalitarians and those that resist them, to induce indifference to European Communist parties' accession to power, or to disrupt security relationships which are essential to maintaining the geopolitical balance. Excuses can be found to deny help to almost any friendly country at the precise moment when it faces its most serious external challenge. If conservatives succeed in unravelling ties with nations on the Left and liberals block relations with nations on the Right, we could find ourselves with no constructive foreign relations at all, except with a handful of industrial democracies. The end result ironically could be the irrelevance of the United States to other nations of the world. A policy of moral advocacy that led to American abdication would surely condemn countless millions to greater suffering, danger, or despair.

Fourth and most fundamentally, we should never forget that the key to successful foreign policy is a sense of proportion. Some of the most serious errors of our foreign policy, both of overcommitment and withdrawal, have occurred when we lost the sense of balance between our interests and our ideals. It was under the banners of moralistic slogans a decade and a half ago that we launched adventures that divided our country and undermined our international position. A few years later young people were parading in front of the White House carrying coffins and candles and accusing their government of loving war; the national leadership was denounced as excessively, indeed imperialistically, involved in the internal affairs of other nations. A few years later still, the government was attacked for sacrificing our ethical values on the altar of détente and being *insufficiently* concerned with the domestic behavior of other nations. Neither we nor the rest of the world can any longer afford such extreme fluctuations.

Human rights policy in this period of American responsibility must strengthen the steady purpose and responsible involvement of the American people. It can do so only if it is presented in the context of a realistic assessment of world affairs and not as the magic cure for the difficulties and shortcomings of mankind's contemporary experience.

The administration is surely right in insisting that human rights is a legitimate and recognized subject of international discourse; it is an object of international legal standards—importantly as a result of American initiatives by administrations of both parties. At the same time, we must recognize that we serve the cause of freedom also by strengthening international security and maintaining ties with other countries defending their independence against external aggression and struggling to overcome poverty, even if their internal structures differ from ours.

We cannot afford to subordinate either concern to the other. Morality without security is ineffectual; security without morality is empty. To establish the relationship and proportion between these goals is perhaps the most profound challenge before our government and our nation.

There is every indication that within the administration rhetoric and capacity for action are being brought increasingly into balance. In an important speech in Athens, Georgia on April 30, 1977, Secretary Vance has wisely pointed out that ''a decision whether and how to act in the cause of human rights is a matter for informed and careful judgment. No mechanistic formula produces an automatic answer.''

Linking Foreign Policy Issues

The inescapable relationship of our human rights objectives with other foreign policy goals is an example of a broader, virtually universal phenomenon of our contemporary world. Foreign policy issues are interrelated— ''linked''—as never before. A consistent, coherent, and moral foreign policy must be grounded in an understanding of the world in which we pursue our goals.

The concept of linkage—the suggestion that we should design and manage our policy with a clear understanding of how changes in one part of the international system affect other parts—was first put forth in 1969 in the context of American-Soviet affairs. We proceeded from the premise that to separate issues into distinct compartments would encourage the Soviet leaders to believe that they could reap the benefits of cooperation in one area, using it as a safety valve, while striving for unilateral advantages elsewhere. We considered this a formula for disaster.

So strong is the pragmatic tradition of American political thought that linkage was widely debated as if it were an idiosyncracy of a particular group of policymakers who chose this approach by an act of will. But linkage comes in two forms: first, when policymakers relate two separate objectives in negotiation, using one as pressure on the other; or by virtue of reality, because in an interdependent world the actions of a major power are inevitably interrelated and have consequences beyond the issue or region immediately concerned. Of these two concepts of linkage, the latter is by far more important. It says, in effect, that significant changes of policy or behavior in one region or on one issue inevitably affect other and wider concerns.

Our policy toward the Soviet Union cannot be treated in isolation from our relations with China; our relations with China, in turn, cannot be effective except to the extent that we maintain the geopolitical balance around the world, by which the People's Republic of China measures our ultimate relevance. Displays of American impotence in one part of the world, such as Southeast Asia or Africa, have a direct effect on our credibility in other parts of the world, such as the Middle East. Our policy toward Rhodesia and Namibia will inevitably determine the prospects of a peaceful evolution in South Africa, and vice-versa. Our posture toward Korea cannot be separated from our interests in Japan and China, and the measures we adopt for one inevitably affect the other. The decision on the B-1 bomber resulted from complex and painful budgetary and technical considerations. I am not here arguing the merits of these considerations, but in the context of the Strategic Arms Limitation talks, the B-1 bomber decision did represent a unilateral, unreciprocated concession. Finally, either our human rights policy has relevance to other areas of national policy— or it has no meaning at all.

Perception of linkage is, in short, synonymous with an overall strategic view. We ignore it only at our peril. It is inherent in the real world. The interrelationship of our interests, across issues and boundaries, exists regardless of the accidents of time or personality; it is not a matter of decision or will but of reality. And it cannot be ended by an act of policy. If we are to have a permanent conception of American foreign policy, there must be an appreciation of the fact that merits of individual actions can be judged only on a wider canvas.

I strongly support President Carter in his fight for ratification of the Panama Canal treaties. I do so on their merits but also because of the profound consequences of a failure to ratify far beyond Panama. A defeat of the treaties would weaken the president's international authority at the beginning of his term. It would suggest to friends and foes around the world that the United States could not deliver on an agreement negotiated by four presidents of both political parties over a period of thirteen years, that it could not perceive its own interests in Western Hemisphere cooperation, and that shifting emotions and institutional stalemates produced erratic behavior in the most powerful country in the world.

Linkage is not a natural concept for Americans, who have traditionally perceived foreign policy as an episodic enterprise. Our bureaucratic organization, divided into regional and functional bureaus, and indeed our academic tradition of specialization, compound this tendency to compartmentalization. And American pragmatism produces a penchant for examining issues separately: to deal with issues individually as if they existed as abstractions without the patience, timing, or sense of political complexity which are so often vital to their achievement; to display our morality in the proclamation of objectives rather than in a commitment to the operational consequences of our actions in an inherently ambiguous environment.

A recognition of the importance of linkage—of the significance and role of the strategic vision to our future foreign policy—thus brings me back to where I began: to the need for patience, continuity, and, above all, for national unity in the conduct of international affairs. This responsibility must be shared by the administration, the opposition, and the public. Modern foreign policy, by its very complexity, does not lend itself to instant successes. In domestic affairs the time frame of new departures is defined by the legislative process; dramatic initiatives may be the only way to launch a new program. In foreign policy the most important initiatives require painstaking preparation; results may be months and years in becoming apparent.

Peace and Freedom

Therefore, we should not demand of the new administration instant results or an unbroken string of early successes; nor should the administration seek such goals if it wishes to avoid a series of stalemates or worse. Foreign policy, if it is to be truly an architectural endeavor, is the art of building for the long term, the careful nurturing of relationships, the elaboration of policies that enhance our options and constrain those of potential opponents. It requires the coherence that can only come from national unity, a strong leadership and a political process that reflects the recognition that we are all—the administration as well as its opponents—part of a permanent national endeavor.

This country has no greater contribution to make in the service of its ideals than to help the world find its way from an era of fear into a time of hope. With our old idealism and our new maturity, we have the opportunity to fulfill the hopes as well as the necessities of a peaceful world. A century ago Abraham Lincoln proclaimed that no nation could long endure ''half slave and half free'' and stirred the conscience of the nation. With a combination of lofty idealism and tough pragmatism, he saved the freedom of this country. With a similar dedication—in a world that is "half slave and half free"—we in this era can be the champion and defender of the cause of liberty.□

CONTRIBUTORS

Elise Boulding ("Children's Rights") is professor of sociology and project director of the Institute of Behavioral Science at the University of Colorado. She is the author of many works on children and women, as well as studies of power and social conflict. Her article is adapted from a chapter of her Transaction book on children's rights.

Adda B. Bozeman ("Understating the Communist Threat") is emeritus professor of international relations and comparative culture history at Sarah Lawrence College. She is the author of numerous books on international politics, culture, and conflict. Her article is adapted from a paper presented to Panel IV of the National Security Affairs Conference at the National Defense University in July 1977.

Tom J. Farer ("Exaggerating the Communist Menace") is professor of law at the Rutgers University School of Law in Camden. He is a member of the Inter-American Human Rights Commission and the author of several monographs and numerous articles on international law and foreign policy. His article is adapted from an anthology forthcoming from the University of Notre Dame Press, *Human Rights and American Foreign Policy*.

A. Belden Fields ("Income Equality as a Human Value") is associate professor of political science at the University of Illinois at Urbana-Champaign. His research focuses on political theory and comparative politics, and he is presently completing a book on Maoism and Trotskyism. He is a member of the recently formed Internat on Human Rights of the International Studies Association.

James Frederick Green ("NGOs") is executive director of the Commission to Study the Organization of Peace. He spent twenty-seven years in the State Department and was executive director of the President's Commission for the Observance of Human Rights Year 1968. He is the author of several books and numerous articles on the subject of human rights.

Chalmers Johnson ("Terror") is professor of political science and chairman of the department at the University of California at Berkeley. Formerly he served as chairman of the University of California's Center for Chinese Studies. He has written on revolution and political violence and was the rapporteur for the State Department's 1976 conference on international terrorism.

Henry A. Kissinger ("Continuity and Change in American Foreign Policy"), former secretary of state, director of the National Security Council, and special assistant to the president for national security affairs, currently teaches at Georgetown University. His article is adapted from the Arthur K. Salomon Lecture delivered at New York University on September 19, 1977.

William Korey ("Final Acts and Final Solutions") is director of the B'nai B'rith International Council and chairman of the Human Rights Committee of the Conference of Nongovernmental Organization Representatives. Formerly he taught at the City College of New York and Columbia University. He has written for both scholarly and popular journals and is the author of several books.

Diane Edwards La Voy ("Foreign Nationals and American Law") is a former staff member of the Senate Select Committee to Study Governmental Operations with Respect to Intelligence Activities. In 1974 she established the Washington Office on Latin America, which assists legislative efforts of a number of church groups. Formerly she served as assistant editor of *Américas*, the Organization of American States magazine.

A. Glenn Mower, Jr. ("Implementing United Nations Covenants") is professor of political science at Hanover College. He is the author of numerous articles on international relations, with emphasis on human rights, in foreign as well as American journals. Formerly he taught at Pennsylvania State and Illinois Wesleyan universities.

John Crothers Pollock ("Reporting Rights Conflicts") is assistant professor of political science and sociology and adjunct professor of journalism and urban communications at Livingston College. He is senior editor of *Studies in Comparative International Development* and the author of *The Politics of Crisis Reporting: American Journalism and Foreign Affairs*.

Alejandro Portes ("Why Illegal Migration? A Human Rights Perspective") is professor of sociology at Duke University. Formerly he taught at the University of Texas at Austin and served as program advisor in the social sciences for the Ford Foundation in Brazil. He is a past contributor to *Society, Studies in Comparative International Development*, and other Transaction publications.

Marcus G. Raskin ("Survival") is founder and codirector of the Institute for Policy Studies/Transnational. He has served as a congressional advisor and as a member of the special staff of the National Security Council and the U.S. Disarmament Delegation to the 1962 Geneva Conference. He is the author of several books on political philosophy, politics, and foreign policy.

David Riesman ("Prospects for Human Rights") is Henry Ford II Professor of the Social Sciences at Harvard University. He is the author of many books on a variety of subjects, most recently the forthcoming *The Perpetual Dream: Experiment and Reform in the American College* (with Gerald Grant). His article is adapted from a commencement address delivered at Williams College on June 5, 1977.

James Lee Robinson, Jr. ("Reporting Rights Conflicts") is assistant professor of political science at Livingston College. His research interests focus on urban and ethnic politics. He is the coauthor of an article on media coverage and the abortion controversy in *Journalism Quarterly*.

Abdul Aziz Said ("Pursuing Human Dignity") is professor of international relations at American University and associate editor of *Society* magazine. He has taught courses on terrorism, ethnicity in world politics, human rights, and others. He was the special guest editor of the human rights issue of *Society*. He is the author of several books on international relations.

Harry M. Scoble ("Human Rights as an International League") is professor of political science at the University of Illinois at Chicago Circle. He has written extensively on American interest groups, community power structures, race and poverty, and international human rights organizations.

Laurie S. Wiseberg ("Human Rights as an International League") is assistant professor of political science at the University of Illinois at Chicago Circle. Her research has focused on international human rights and disaster relief.

DATE DUE